TRACING YOUR ANCESTORS FROM 1066 TO 1837

FAMILY HISTORY FROM PEN & SWORD

TRACING YOUR ANCESTORS FROM 1066 TO 1837

A Guide for Family Historians

Jonathan Oates

Pen & Sword
FAMILY HISTORY

First published in Great Britain in 2012
and reprinted in 2013, 2015, 2017, 2019, 2020 and 2021 by
Pen & Sword FAMILY HISTORY
An imprint of Pen & Sword Books Ltd
Yorkshire – Philadelphia

ISBN: 978 1 84884 609 8

A CIP catalogue record for this book is available from the British Library

Typeset in Palatino and Optima by Phoenix Typesetting, Auldgirth, Dumfriesshire
Printed and bound in England by CPI Group (UK) Ltd, Croydon, CR0 4YY

Pen & Sword Books Limited incorporates the imprints of Atlas, Archaeology,
Aviation, Discovery, Family History, Fiction, History, Maritime, Military, Military
Classics, Politics, Select, Transport, True Crime, Air World, Frontline Publishing, Leo
Cooper, Remember When, Seaforth Publishing, The Praetorian Press, Wharncliffe
Local History, Wharncliffe Transport, Wharncliffe True Crime and White Owl.

For a complete list of Pen & Sword titles please contact PEN & SWORD BOOKS
LIMITED 47 Church Street, Barnsley, South Yorkshire, S70 2AS, England E-mail:
enquiries@pen-and-sword.co.uk • Website: www.pen-and-sword.co.uk
Or
PEN AND SWORD BOOKS
1950 Lawrence Rd, Havertown, PA 19083, USA E-mail: Uspen-and-
sword@casematepublishers.com Website: www.penandswordbooks.com

CONTENTS

ACKNOWLEDGEMENTS

I wish to acknowledge the assistance of Ruth Costello, Caroline Lang, John Coulter and John Gauss in the production of this book, all of whom are knowledgeable in family and/or local history. They took the time and trouble to read the text and to make helpful suggestions. I would also like to acknowledge Paul Lang for once again putting his considerable postcard collection at my disposal.

I dedicate this book to my former tutor, and a renowned medievalist, Professor Brian R Kemp.

INTRODUCTION

Family history is a fast-growing hobby in the twenty-first century. Many sources are available online on sites such as findmypast.com and ancestry.co.uk. Family history magazines abound and family history societies exist throughout the country. Popular programmes on television have ensured that family history is very much in vogue.

However, much of this concentrates on the last two centuries. The reasons are straightforward. First, the key sources for family history are oral tradition, the census and civil registration records. Most people will know about their parents and grandparents or can be told about them by living family members, and this is always the best place to start your ancestral research. The national census began in 1801, it is true, but it was only in 1841 that the recording of names was required. Civil registration, which recorded births, marriages and deaths, only began in 1837. All these sources can provide much basic information about names, dates and places. Secondly, these sources are available without you having to leave the comfort of your own home because the census and indexes to civil registration can be viewed online. Thirdly, other key sources, such as First World War soldiers' records and medals can also be seen online. Other published sources, such as newspapers, telephone directories, electoral registers and street directories (almost all of which are chiefly products of the increasingly democratic and literate Victorian and post-Victorian era) are easily accessed at borough and county record offices and some are online, too. Finally they are all written in English.

It is very common for many people to trace their ancestors to the Victorian age using these sources. After that many people become stuck. Research becomes more difficult, especially if the surname searched for is a common one. There are less archives surviving because fewer were created, for the state at the national level took less interest in people's lives than it has since and there was a far smaller bureaucracy. The manuscripts which do exist are more difficult to read and they can often be in Latin. There is more of an emphasis on the social elite than the majority of the population (i.e. the bulk of our ancestors). Finally, most of the earlier material is not online.

However, there is no need to give up hope. There are many sources available for our ancestors prior to 1837 and the aim of this book is to illuminate and illustrate them so they can yield their secrets. The book takes

The Muniment Room, Guildhall, London. Paul Lang's collection.

1066 as its starting date because there is scarcely any documentation about individuals other than monarchs and the nobility before the Norman Conquest. In any case, very few people can trace their family back prior to 1066, because most of the Saxon male elite were killed in that year. Moreover, the Anglo-Saxon state did not have the type of government which created many records.

The two major record creating bodies after the Conquest were the church and the state, though the two were often one. Both were national bodies which operated throughout the kingdom. They made records about the people in their jurisdictions, as regards the law, finance, military service, land ownership, religious affiliation, political loyalty and other important areas of life, including sexual morality. It is these records that this book will discuss. We will see what exists, where it is located, the information contained therein and how best to get the most from it. This book does not promise that it will enable a reader to find out what their ancestors were doing in 1066, but it will, hopefully, enable him or her to push back the chronological borders of their knowledge of their English ancestors.

This is not a book aimed at the beginner in family history. It is for those who have already explored the familiar twentieth- and nineteenth-century sources. The envisaged readership is those who know all about their family history back to the beginning of the Victorian age, and who want to dig deeper. You will already know the names of your ancestors of the 1830s and 1840s and want to know about their ancestors. Two tips to begin with. Start with the ancestors you know about and then work carefully backward. Do not go straight to the Domesday Book or another medieval survey and start searching there. Second, think about which institutions of church and state your ancestor might have come into contact with and so which ones would have reason to record their activities.

This is the author's second book about family history. His other specialisms are criminal and military history. He has also worked in record offices in the north of England and in London since 1991, as well as having worked on his and his wife's family history, so has a strong knowledge of sources and of assisting in researchers' enquiries. Hopefully this book will help others.

One abbreviation used throughout this book is TNA, The National Archives, the single most important source of information for family historians.

It should also be noted that book covers family history in England, but much of what lies herein will be applicable to the other constituent parts of the British Isles. For detailed studies of Scotland and Ireland see the relevant titles in the Pen and Sword Family History series.

Chapter 1

THE STATE AND CHURCH, 1066–1837

Histories of England are commonplace. This chapter offers a brief synopsis, concentrating on social, religious, economic and administrative matters. In order to understand the sources for researchers in these centuries, we need to know a little about them. This will not be a concise history of England in this period, but rather a history of its administrative institutions and how these evolved over the centuries. It was these institutions that created the records that supply us with the information about our ancestors.

Medieval England, 1066–1485

England, as a political entity with defined borders, came about in the tenth century, with the defeat of the Viking incursions, at least temporarily, the establishment of borders with Wales and Scotland, and the unification of the Saxon kingdoms into one, under the House of Wessex. Counties were beginning to be formed in the seventh and eighth centuries, chiefly in the south of England. After 1066, others were formed and these thirty-nine counties became the administrative building blocks of the English state up until the 1970s. They varied considerably in size and population, with Yorkshire, Lincolnshire and Devon being the largest and Rutland and Middlesex being the smallest. However the latter contained the most populous city in the country, London. In the Middle Ages, the county's chief secular officer in the king's interest was the sheriff, responsible for law and order, and for many is best, if unfairly, represented by the Sheriff of Nottingham in the Robin Hood stories.

Religion was a major influence on the life of our ancestors. Arguably it was the most important and it is essential that readers should remember this. Christianity was re-established in England in the seventh and eight centuries and the old pagan gods were eventually vanquished. All men owed religious allegiance to the Pope, of course, until the Protestant Reformation of the sixteenth century. It is difficult to exaggerate the power of the medieval church over all the kingdom's souls. There were two

1

Site of the Battle of Hastings, 1066 Author.

provinces, York and Canterbury, and these were subdivided into dioceses (which rarely equated to the county system), then archdeaconries, then parishes (which, again, did not equate with manors). As well as the diocesan system, there were also the monastic houses of the Benedictine and Cistercian orders, to name but two of the more numerous. They maintained numerous abbeys, priories, monasteries, chantries and chapels throughout the country. In 1216 there were 700 religious houses and 13,000 monks and nuns; their numbers increased throughout the century. This was partly because of the increase in numbers of friaries. Abbots were leading tenants of the king and held many manors. Monasteries also maintained hospitals and libraries as well as being centres for the worship of God. The parish priest, by contrast, was a humble fellow; he farmed the land he held from the lord of the manor and was rarely celibate, until reforms later in the eleventh century.

Although the Norman Conquest resulted in a new monarch and a new aristocracy supplanting the old one (4,000 Saxon thegns were replaced by 200 barons), much remained the same. This was the feudal system in which the monarch was landholder in chief (under God) and his leading followers were his chief tenants, both nobility and churchmen, who held (not owned, at least in theory) land from him. This would usually be scattered throughout the kingdom rather than being one substantial swathe of territory. They had lesser tenants and so the process went downwards. In return for such land, the tenant owed his immediate superior service, often military, but increasingly as time went by, financial.

English society was overwhelmingly rural, with very few towns and cities. Most people lived and worked on the land in manors. The major groupings therein were the villeins, who held 45% of land and made up 41% of the population, then cottars, who held a mere 5% of land but made up about 32% of the population. Then there were the landless, about 9% of the population. At the other end of the scale were freemen, making up 14% of the population, but holding 20% of land, and, of course, the tiny elite of barons and bishops. Most people worked in farming and fishing; the only industry of any importance was cloth. Very few people lived in towns; London had about 40,000 residents in the fifteenth century and most towns and cities counted residents in their thousands.

Government and society in the Middle Ages were far different to what they are today. National government was in the hands of the King and his council, with the former the most important figure in the political world. He could declare war, embark on diplomacy, choose his own servants and levy taxes. His wealth and powers of patronage were extensive and so he could reward his supporters and promise rewards to others whose loyalty he required. He was not absolute, of course, and had to choose his friends and his policies carefully. Disastrous decisions and bad luck resulted in Edward II and Henry VI being deposed and murdered. The monarchy was not always hereditary at this time, though it often was. From 1154 to 1485 the monarchs were members of the House of Plantagenet.

Central government was very minimal and it was also very itinerant; the monarch moved about the country and his government moved with him. Yet, despite the growth in officials, there were still relatively few of what we would call civil servants. By the end of the fifteenth century government had become fixed at Westminster. Far more of the day-to-day administration was in the hands of urban corporations and manorial courts. Health and education were not the province of government.

Law and order was a major preoccupation of the monarch and his government. In the twelfth century, Henry II instituted the assizes system of courts which was to endure until 1971. These resulted in itinerant judges touring circuits, each made up of a number of adjacent counties, twice a year, to hear cases of serious crime.

England's major wars were with the Welsh in the thirteenth century, resulting in the conquest of Wales, then less successfully with the Scots, then with the French in the Hundred Years War of 1337–1453. There were also civil wars, such as that in Stephen's reign, Simon de Montfort's baronial wars in the next century, and the wars between York and Lancaster in the fifteenth, not to mention rebellions against Henry II, Edward II and Henry IV. All these resulted in demands for financial subsidies as well as levies of men to fight either at home or abroad. Troops were raised when needed and disbanded when wars were over; there was no standing army or navy.

Parliament emerged in the thirteenth century, but was primarily a court

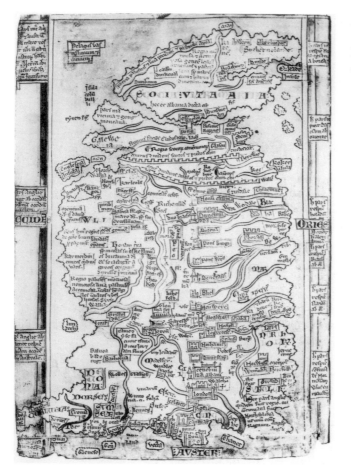

Map of Britain, 1250.
Paul Lang's collection.

of law rather than a fiscal institution. Taxation was not required on an annual basis, but for extraordinary expenditure, which usually meant paying for war. In peacetime, the monarch was expected to live using his resources such as Crown lands, customs dues, feudal incidents and the profits of justice, and these provided the bulk of his revenue. Parliament had brief sittings and in the second half of the fifteenth century only met once every three years.

England's population fluctuated greatly. With between 1 and 2 million inhabitants in 1066, it then grew steadily in the next centuries, perhaps reaching 5–7 million by 1300, but was cut savagely in the fourteenth century due to the Black Death. Possibly a third or half of the population died. By the end of the Middle Ages, numbers had only reached about 2.5 million. The population was becoming increasingly literate and French, the

Medieval peasants harvesting. Paul Lang's collection.

language of government since the Conquest, was replaced by English in the fourteenth century.

By the end of the Middle Ages the English state had incorporated Wales as a principality and claimed sovereignty over Ireland and Scotland, though most of the French possessions of the Norman and Plantagenet monarchies of the eleventh and twelfth centuries had been lost. It was an increasingly self-confident, though small, nation.

Tudor and Stuart England, 1485–1714

Henry VII, the first of the Tudor monarchs, following his decisive victory at Bosworth and the death in battle of his predecessor, Richard III, continued the attempts of Edward IV to strengthen the monarchy, both financially and judicially, though there was still no standing army or police force. Henry introduced legal and judicial methods such as the Court of Star Chamber to rule England and to make the Crown stronger and richer than the chief landowners. Tudor government saw a shift from the medieval towards the more bureaucratic form of government which we are more accustomed to now, but we should not exaggerate this revolution as much stayed the same.

The key change was the relation between church and state which culminated in the Dissolution of the monastic houses in the 1530s and made the monarch rather than the Pope the head of the church. This led to the same individual being at the head of both church and state. At the bottom level of both was the parish, and its powers rose throughout the century. It also

5

led to a major redistribution of landed power as monastic land was bought or given to the nobility and the gentry, the latter becoming increasingly an important force in politics.

Henry VIII was the head of a Catholic Church; however, he was his own 'Pope'. It was during his son's brief reign that the Protestant Reformation made state-sponsored progress. Although this was interrupted by his Catholic sister Mary's equally brief reign, a compromise of sorts was reached under Elizabeth. The Church of England became Protestant, though not of a radical brand as desired by some. Equally, the Catholic faith was under attack. This was increasingly the case as the century drew on and England became involved in wars with foreign Catholic powers, chiefly Spain.

Religious radicalism had helped lead to the Reformation, but was also a result of it, too. There were many Protestants who refused to acknowledge the sovereignty of the monarchy. Initially these were termed Puritans. Their fortunes waxed and waned over this period and perhaps reached their zenith in the 1650s when the Anglican Church, deprived of monarch and bishops, was at its weakest. Yet the Restoration of 1660 resulted in Nonconformists being penalized, as they had been since 1559. They could not worship legally and faced fines and imprisonment. The Bill of Rights of 1689 led to a limited toleration of Nonconformist worship, though full political, educational and civil equality was not achieved until the early nineteenth century. Not everyone turned towards Protestantism in any form. There were minorities who clung to Catholicism, especially in parts of northern England. As with Nonconformists, their political and civic rights were limited, as were their religious ones.

Parliament grew in strength as a political entity in these centuries, though this was not pre-ordained as monarchs had ruled without it in 1629–1640, 1681–5 and 1685–8, and it was, ironically, much reduced in power during the Commonwealth years. Parliament's importance was not merely legislative but fiscal. The monarch could no longer live without direct taxation as the cost of government had risen, especially if he or she wanted to maintain a standing army and conduct an interventionist foreign policy. By 1689 it was an indispensable political institution.

This is not to say that the monarchy's powers were vastly reduced. They were still expected to rule as well as reign. They could declare war or conduct diplomacy. They could choose their own ministers. They had an immense amount of patronage at their disposal. However they had to work in partnership with Parliament; not always an easy task, but by the time of William III (1689–1702), they could do so without the major quarrels which had been the case under the earlier Stuarts and which had led to civil war in 1642.

Local administration increasingly passed into the hands of the quarter sessions and the parish and away from the sheriff and the manor, though these institutions remained. Social and economic legislation was entrusted to these bodies, for the Crown had no paid centralized bureaucracy. Relief of the poor became a foremost priority of this legislation. All this gave immense local power to the gentry.

The chief secular figure in the counties was the Lord Lieutenant, a politically reliable nobleman, who replaced the sheriff, whose office became more ceremonial than practical. He was the monarch's representative and an important link between the counties and the court. He was also a key military figure, for it was he who was responsible for the militia, the country's military force for home defence.

Britain was not a major European power in this period, except in the 1650s and from 1689. Because of this, there was no standing army in England until the later seventeenth century. Men were raised to fight wars and then were disbanded after they were over, as had always been the case. However, after England's most devastating wars – the Civil Wars of 1642–51 – a permanent army was created. Charles II disbanded most of the Commonwealth forces, but retained a few regiments, and these, added to

Henry VIII (1509–1547). Paul Lang's collection.

7

the troops he brought from exile, became Britain's first regular army kept in being in peacetime, chiefly as garrisons at home and abroad.

The post-1660 army was small by Continental standards, but once England joined the struggle of the great powers there from 1689 onwards, it grew. Officers became increasingly professional and long-serving, especially under the Hanoverians. Troops served overseas at an increasing level in garrisons in Britain's expanding Empire, though forces were also employed at home, especially as there was no national police force. The Royal Navy increasingly became both larger and more professional, especially from the mid-seventeenth century.

Population rapidly increased, from 2.25 million in 1526 to 4.1 million in 1603; a large increase indeed, which led to strain on resources, mounting prices and an increase in poverty in the late sixteenth century. Yet most survived plague and war and by 1700, England's population stood at 5 million. This was still a rural society, with few towns of any significant size outside London, and communication was still basic.

Britain was becoming a united political entity in these centuries. England and Wales were formally joined in 1536, following the medieval dynastic link. England and Scotland shared a monarch from 1603, and in 1707, the Act of Union brought Scotland's existence as an independent political entity to an end. Successful wars resulted, by 1713, in Britain being recognized as one of the great powers of Europe as well as one of the world's leading maritime and colonial nations.

Hanoverian England, 1714–1837

The Elector of Hanover became George I in 1714. There was a question over his dynasty's survival in the face of threats from the exiled Stuarts. This led to major rebellions in both England and Scotland in 1715, but these were defeated within months. Unlike the previous century the country then enjoyed internal peace, apart from the Jacobite rebellion of 1745.

Major changes were occurring in society and economy, too. The 'Agricultural Revolution' accelerated change in the rural economy, with increasing amounts of arable land being enclosed by Acts of Parliament, and thus changing the face of the countryside forever. Farmers began to experiment with innovative methods of growing crops, resulting in higher yields. Elsewhere, industrial growth was being seen, especially in the West Riding of Yorkshire and in the Midlands as industry became less concentrated in small-scale operations and began to be big business as factories were first created. The impact of these developments should not be exaggerated as they took decades to become widespread.

Communication also underwent a lengthy revolution in the Georgian period, and this facilitated industrial growth, too. Roads were improved by turnpike trusts and so travel was quicker. Canals were dug in the latter half of the eighteenth century, thus easing the transportation of goods. Finally, just as our period was ending, steam power was harnessed to bring about the world's first railways. All these developments assisted in the process known to historians as the Industrial Revolution which was transforming Britain into the 'Workshop of the World' and thus into the modern age. The textile industry was the most important, with cotton becoming dominant by 1810. Coal and iron production also soared, thanks to improved techniques and inventions.

Population increased, from about 5 million in 1700, to 8.3 million a century later and then to 13.1 million in 1831. London's population topped one million. Death rates were falling and birth rates rose. Yet in 1801, only 30% of the population lived in towns, and most of these in towns with less than 10,000 people. Most of these towns were not industrialized, but maritime or dockyard towns, or regional centres.

Politically and constitutionally, the authority of Parliament rose relative to that of the Crown, albeit by evolutionary means. Royal patronage declined in the later eighteenth century. Under George IV the prestige of the monarchy declined, too. The Reform Act of 1832 led to a redistribution of seats as well as an increase in the electorate; the first such changes to the constitution since the experiments of the Commonwealth. Political parties began to become more recognizable, with the Whigs and Tories being more than abusive labels for the factions of the late seventeenth century. New towns became constituencies in their own right. Radicalism emerged as a political force in the 1760s, and continued as a major extra-parliamentary force from thereon, partly aided by the growth of national and local newspapers.

England had several forms of Protestantism in 1714, and their number grew in the century. The Wesley brothers founded Methodism which became the largest Nonconformist grouping. Despite popular fears about Catholicism, the decline of Jacobitism as a political danger eventually led to anti-Catholic legislation being repealed, so that by the end of the eighteenth century Catholics could worship in peace and Catholic priests no longer feared legal prosecution. This led to a reduction in the influence of the established Anglican Church, yet this institution remained a powerful force into the nineteenth century.

Much remained the same. The counties continued to be ruled by the quarter sessions. However, central government grew in power relative to them, with the creation of the New Poor Law in 1834, which led to a decline in the administrative importance of the parishes. In 1833 the first government educational grant was made and in 1829 the Metropolitan Police was formed. The old order was changing, but at an evolutionary pace.

By 1815 Britain had emerged as the world's greatest power by virtue of its financial, economic, military and naval strength. The American colonies had been lost in 1781, but much had been retained, including Canada and islands in the West Indies. There had been new acquisitions elsewhere, and Britain, through the East India Company, had become the leading power in India, having ousted the French.

Generally speaking there were several key differences between the centuries between 1066 and 1837 and the twenty-first century. England was far less densely populated and the majority of its residents lived in the countryside and earned their living from agriculture. The authority of the monarch and the church, as well as the nobility and the gentry was far greater. Most people had at best a fairly rudimentary education and led shorter lives. Central government had a far more limited role in most peoples' lives. This, then, was the England of 1066–1837, centuries of great change, in which your ancestors lived. It is now time to investigate how you can discover who they were and what they did.

Chapter 2

ARCHEPISCOPAL AND EPISCOPAL RECORDS

The role of the church in our ancestors' lives up until the nineteenth century is difficult to overestimate and was on a scale unthinkable to most now living in more secular times. Much of this power in educational and legal affairs was transferred to the state in the nineteenth century. We shall examine the higher echelons of the church in this chapter; the lower levels will be dealt with in the next.

With the reintroduction of Christianity to England in 597, the Church established itself slowly across the country. England was divided into two provinces with a total of seventeen dioceses. These were the province of York with four dioceses, which included the northern counties of Northumberland, Durham, Yorkshire, Cumberland, Westmorland, Lancashire, Cheshire and Nottinghamshire. The larger province, was that of Canterbury, which included the remainder of the country. Each was headed by an archbishop and that of Canterbury was the senior of the two. Neither was head of the church in England; up to the Henrican reformation of the sixteenth century this was the Pope, then the monarch thereafter when church and state fused and changed from Catholic to Protestant.

Beneath the level of the province was the diocese, which was headed by a bishop. Diocese was not the same as county. Thus the diocese of Durham included Northumberland as well as Durham, and the diocese of Carlisle consisted of Cumberland and Westmorland. At the Reformation, six more dioceses were created but one, Westminster, only lasted a few years; a more permanent one was Chester, created in 1542 out of part of the diocese of Lichfield and it included Lancashire, Cheshire and part of Westmorland. Dioceses varied considerably in size and income. Durham was one of the richest in the eighteenth century, Carlisle and Rochester two of the poorest. Archbishops and bishops sat in the House of Lords and were important territorial and political figures with access to the monarch, as well as being key figures in the ecclesiastical world. They were appointed by the monarch, though the government took an increasing interest especially from the eighteenth century.

The next tier of administration was the archdeaconry; there were a

Statue of George Abbot, Archbishop of Canterbury, 2011. Author.

number of these in each diocese, totalling fifty-eight in the country in the Middle Ages, and this number varied enormously with Lincoln possessing eight, York five and Carlisle one. Archdeacons had to inspect the parishes in order to ensure that they were well run. Provinces, dioceses and archdeaconries all ran their own religious courts. The lowest level was the parish.

Ecclesiastical Courts

Ordinary people came under the jurisdiction of these institutions. Church courts were established in Saxon times, but their role was more sharply defined under the Normans, clearly separating their and the Crown's judicial authority. Until 1858 (apart from a brief interlude under the Commonwealth), authority over probate was in the hands of the clerical courts. Secondly, these courts dealt with a variety of offences relating to religion and morals, if the two could be seen as separate, up to 1860.

These courts dealt with a variety of matters, though these tend to be less well known now. The Church was concerned, naturally enough, with Christian morality and was empowered to deal with those who transgressed its boundaries. Because these courts dealt with sexual matters, such as adultery, fornication, divorce and incest, they have been named the bawdy courts. Other offences included slander, the refusal to pay tithes, non attendance

Bishop's staff of authority. Paul Lang's collection.

at church and Easter offerings. Witchcraft was dealt with by the church courts up to the sixteenth century when it became a civil criminal offence. Suits could be brought against clergymen, too, by both the laity and fellow clergy. Those damaging church property also fell into their orbit. It has been estimated that about a tenth of our medieval ancestors were brought before these courts.

Going before them was no laughing matter. Chaucer's archdeacon relished in the execution of the penal aspects of his role:

> An erchedeken, a man of heigh degree
> That boldely dide execucion,
> In punisshinge of fournicacion,
> Of Wicchecraft, and eek of bauderye,
> Of diffamacioun and avoutrye.

Usually the initial step was for the churchwardens of the parish to inform the court of any parishioners who had caused offence.

Either clergy or lay people would bring cases before the courts on these matters. A judge, a senior churchman, would preside. Proceedings would be recorded in the Act Books, along with the results. Undisputed cases were resolved quickly but disputed ones involved the calling of advocates for both parties. If plenary procedure was followed, written pleas and statements were given. The plaintiff would provide the judge with his case for the judge to decide whether the court could deal with it. If so, he issued a citation on their behalf for the defendant to answer. This resulted in a number of statements for the defendant to answer. Witnesses would then make written statements against these points. Once the judge decided there was enough information from both sides, he would resolve the case and make a judgment. Costs would then be awarded. There was also summary court procedure, used in criminal cases only, when the evidence provided would be oral.

Those found guilty could be sentenced to a number of humiliating punishments. Public penance was a common sentence. Those found guilty had to stand in a designated public place for a set number of occasions, often on market days or on Sundays, and for a designated time, with a notice about their person stating their offence. Once this penance was completed, the offender would be advised to sin no more. The final deterrent to any proving obdurate was to threaten excommunication, though several warnings were given before so final a step was taken. In a world where Christianity was almost universal, this was no small threat.

Church court records are usually found in Act Books at the diocesan record office; those of Canterbury are found at Canterbury Cathedral Archives, those for York at the Borthwick Institute, and those of the dioceses either with the county record office or the cathedral itself. They tend to be less used than wills because they have not been indexed, as have most wills, and so searching for ancestors will be a lengthy task and quite possibly fruitless if your ancestors led sexually blameless lives. Of course, up to 1733 the documents will be in Latin, a further bar to some researchers. Act Books summarize a case to be taken before an ecclesiastical court. They give the depositions of witnesses, which include the witness' name, occupation, age, residence and perhaps information about their previous residence and work. There may also be cause papers, detailing arguments and evidence used in court. They were most active in the sixteenth and seventeenth centuries.

Some Act Books have been published, chiefly for the eleventh to the thirteenth centuries, by the English Episcopal Acta by the Oxford University Press and the British Academy (see www.oup.co.uk for a list of those published). Some have also been published by county record societies and by the Selden Society.

Useful guides are C R Chapman, *Ecclesiastical Courts: Their Officials and their Records* (1992), Ann Tarver, *Church Court Records* (1994) and Martin Ingram's *Church Courts: Sex and Marriage in England, 1570–1640* (1987).

Wills

It is better known that these courts also dealt with probate. Wills express the final testament of an individual and are necessary to avoid unnecessary disputes by legitimizing the last wishes of the deceased. The practice of bequeathing goods originates from Saxon times, but wills as we know them do not start until the twelfth century. The earliest which survive date from the fourteenth century.

They would be made before witnesses and could often be formulated months or years before death. The will would be proved before the appropriate court, usually shortly after the death of the testator, so it helps date the death. They are potentially very important documents for the researcher. This is because they show how wealthy an individual was, and what he or (rarely in this period) she owned, and their property and goods, as well as money and other assets, may be listed in some detail. It will also list those family members, friends and organizations (perhaps the church or a charity) to whom these assets were bequeathed. Of course, not everyone left a will. Married women only did so rarely because on marriage their goods passed to their husband. Spinsters, of course, could make wills, as did Jane Austen who died in 1817.

There were documents called administrations (often known as 'admons') for those who died intestate, and for whom the court had to grant powers to another to make the division of the estate. A friend or relative of the deceased had to apply to the court for these and often had to enter into a bond that he would settle all the deceased's debts and make up a true inventory of the deceased's goods. Administrations are to be found with wills in diocesan record offices. Information about the administrator is also given.

In the seventeenth century, inventories were commonplace and where they exist can be very informative indeed. They tend to exist in large numbers from the sixteenth to the eighteenth century. The court would appoint executors to make an inventory. Goods, including furniture, tools and agricultural produce and livestock would all be included.

Prior to the twentieth century, perhaps only about 10% of the population made provision for their goods and chattels after death. Yet wills can be found for quite poor people, as well as for the obviously affluent, so they are always worth looking for. Finding them can be tricky however.

This is because there were a number of courts operating in each county. The two most important were those of the archbishops, and these had superior jurisdiction to all other courts in the country. Of these the largest was the Prerogative Court of Canterbury, often abbreviated to PCC (not to be confused with Parochial Church Council, which originated in 1920). This dealt with predominantly wills proved in the south and Midlands of England (and Wales), though not wholly so; if a testator owned land in both provinces, it is worth checking both prerogative courts. They cover wills from 1383 to 1858, numbering over a million. They are located at TNA. However, access is straightforward. PCC wills can be searched for online on the TNA's website, by simply typing in the testator's name, together with year of death if known. If you don't know whether someone made a will, you can check easily and quickly, and for free, so if nothing is found there is no loss; and you can then search another probate jurisdiction if desired.

If the name of the individual sought for is located, you have two options if you want to progress. You can either pay the fee and be sent an electronic version of the will, which is certainly the quickest method. Or if you can visit TNA, you can see the record online for free. However, depending on your time and ability to read medieval handwriting, you may need to take a printout in any case.

The other prerogative court was that of York, covering the counties of the province as listed above. These are held at the Borthwick Institute, part of the University of York, but indexes to those for the Prerogative Court of York, 1688–1858, all Yorkshire peculiars and all Yorkshire wills prior to

Durham Cathedral, 2009 Author.

1500 can be seen on the website British Origins. The full text can then be ordered once the individual has been found.

Apart from these courts, each diocese had its own consistory court. This was used by testators who had property in more than one archdeaconry within the same diocese, but it also administered wills in parishes exempt from the archdeacon's remit. The actual court was in part of the cathedral, and if you visit Chester cathedral you can still see the court. There were also commissary courts, which were under the bishop's control, though these operated only in one archdeaconry in the diocese.

The lowest level of courts was the archdeaconry courts. There were varying numbers of these in each diocese. The smallest dioceses, such as Oxford, had but one. In the diocese of Exeter there were four: Barnstaple, Exeter, Cornwall and Totnes. They tended to deal with estates which were solely in one archdeaconry, usually small ones. Finally, there were the peculiars. These were single parishes or groups of parishes in a diocese, not necessarily adjacent, which were exempt from the archdeaconry and consistory court jurisdictions. Instead, wills there were dealt with by someone else, perhaps a locally appointed official or perhaps by a clergyman from the cathedral.

It is impossible to be specific about the location of these archives or to list their accessibility and the available finding aids and lists. Most of them are held at the county record office because that is usually the diocesan record office, so you should contact them in the first place. Remember that some wills proved prior to 1733 will be in Latin, though by no means all. Because there are numerous courts dealing with wills, you should check all of them, though wealthy individuals will have property in numerous parishes and counties, so will be more likely to have their wills proved in one of the two prerogative courts, with the less rich being dealt with by the archdeaconry courts. The best reference work for locating wills is Gibson's *Wills and Where to Find them*, which gives the reader a county by county guide. However, British Origins has indexes to a numerous wills online other than those for Yorkshire and their collection is growing to form a National Wills Index pre-1858.

Wills vary considerably in length. Jane Austen's is a lengthy paragraph but Sir Robert Walpole's is three pages long and by no means the most lengthy. Most tend to be set out in a formulaic manner, so once you have seen a few, that will be of great help. The testator would often commend their soul to God, and make reference to burial. There may then follow charitable bequests. Then the disposal of land and goods begins. The immediate family would then be listed, followed by more distant relatives, perhaps. Finally executors would be listed, people whom the testator nominated to ensure that the will was brought before the court. The following English translation of a fifteenth century will provides an example.

I Hugh Cole of Northolt.

I wish to be buried in the churchyard at Northall.

Item:- I leave to the altar of the said church xijd.

Item:- I leave to John Cole of Greenford 6s 4d.

Item:- I leave for prayers for my soul to be said at the church of Greenford, 20d.

Item:- I leave to Northall church a chest, for the parish, to be made by John Shrubbe and John Shepard.

Item:- I leave to Northall church a vestment.

Item:- I leave a cow to the same church.

Item:- I leave a cow to Simon Randolfe.

Note that all wills between 1653 and 1660 were proved by the PCC, when the Commonwealth had abolished the bishops as well as the monarchy. Only a minority of people (about a third to a quarter of adult men) made wills in any case, and very few prior to the sixteenth century. Much that is in a will, such as lengthy preambles, may be of limited interest, but even these may give a clue to the deceased's religious feelings. Finally, just because certain family members are not named may not be evidence of a family falling out – it is possible that they may have been previously provided for, perhaps on marriage.

Bishops' Registers

From the thirteenth to the seventeenth century, written registry books were kept by the dioceses. Apart from recording grants for repairs to churches and the consecration of new churches, they also refer to people. There are references to clerical appointments, church court business, estate and financial management, licences, dispensations and visitations. Significant figures in the diocese's business might be noted. These would include benefactors and witnesses to transactions involving the diocese. Deaths and marriages of these people could be included.

However, the use of such archives is hit and miss. First they are almost all written in Latin. They are arranged chronologically and without an index. Thirdly the information provided is very variable. On the positive side, some of these registers have been transcribed and published and are so easy to use. The Canterbury and York Society has taken a lead in the production of these, though other institutions have also done so. Dorothy Owen's *Medieval Records in Print* (1982) should help in tracking them down.

Licences

The church licensed individuals to practise in a wide variety of occupations, including schoolmasters, doctors and midwives. They were required to swear their allegiance to the establishedchurch. John Lucas, a Leeds schoolmaster, had to apply to the diocese's chancellor in 1714 to have his licence confirmed. Two churchwardens and the vicar of the church he attended had to confirm that he received the holy sacrament following the Anglican Church's rites.

Marriage licences could also be granted from bishops' courts. If two people wanted to marry but did not want to go through the process of having banns read out three times in church, or they wanted to marry in a church in a parish in which neither was resident, they could apply for a licence. This was not inexpensive so was relatively rare. It occurred in the case of Thomas Smethurst's first marriage in Kennington in 1828. Smethurst (1804–73) was a bigamist and possible wife poisoner.

Visitations

Ministers and churchwardens were asked at regular intervals by the bishop or archdeacon about the state of their parish. Names of Catholics and Dissenters in the parish may be given; otherwise there is useful information about the parish given there. Those for York for 1743 and 1764 have been published by the *Yorkshire Archaeological Society Record Series*.

Bishop's Palace, Wells. Paul Lang's collection.

Records of Religious Houses

So far we have examined the archives of the two provinces and the dioceses. Yet we should not forget the hundreds of religious houses swept away by the Dissolution of the Monasteries in the 1530s. These created records, too, and since they were great landowners and dealt with many people are not insignificant. However, the dissolution did result in many of their records being destroyed or lost. Some do survive, at TNA, BL and elsewhere. To find which institutions were near where your ancestors lived, try Knowles and Hadcock, *Medieval Religious Houses in England and Wales* (1971).

Their archives include cartularies. These are copies of charters which were in the institution's possession and describe land given to that institution. Then there are chronicles, a list of which has been compiled by the Mississippi State University (www.chronica.msstate.edu/chronica). They often refer to local events and people, so have clear genealogical value. Although written in Latin and often in private hands, some have been transcribed and published in the Rolls series of 255 volumes which cover the period up to the sixteenth century. These should be available at university libraries. County history societies have transcribed them too. Papal Registers are another possible source, and these volumes have been calendared as 'Calendar of Entries in the Papal Registers relating to Great Britain and Ireland, 1198–1513'. Another volume concerns petitions to the Pope from 1342 to 1419. Marriages between members of the aristocracy are often mentioned, especially where there was concern about close relatives marrying.

Don't forget that cathedrals will contain many monuments and vaults, with varying details of those buried there. There may even be a brass or sarcophagus if you are extremely fortunate. Usually these will be from the upper echelons of sacred and secular society, but if your ancestor is amongst them there may be useful information therein – as well as being an excellent subject for a photograph or rubbing, but do ask permission from the cathedral authorities first.

Other diocesan records relate to clergymen, such as books listing their ordinations and institutions to benefices. The Church also ran schools, such as the charity schools in the eighteenth century, though records rarely listed pupils, but chiefly schoolmasters and benefactors. Finally, don't forget that the Church was a significant holder of lands and kept many estate records including surveys and other records relating to tenants.

Apart from wills, most researchers do not often come into contact with the archives of the Church above parish level. However these archives should not be dismissed. Although the Act Books will not be your first port of call, an inspection of any published volumes for the diocese(s) your ancestors dwelt in would not be a difficult or time-consuming process. If your ancestors were teachers in the seventeenth and eighteenth centuries you should certainly seek out the certificate confirming their adherence to Anglicanism.

Chapter 3

CHURCH RECORDS, PART 2: THE PARISH

From the sixteenth to the nineteenth century, the most important single institution in the life of the majority of the population was the parish. This was not just because of the religious significance of the parish, as important as that was, but because legislation passed under the Tudors led to the parish being an important secular institution, too, superseding the manor. The parish was the lowest administrative unit of both

The Round church, Cambridge, 1900s. Paul Lang's collection.

church and state, and by the eighteenth century there were about 10,000 of them in England.

Parishes have their origin in the late Saxon and the Norman centuries and most had been formed by 1200, as secular magnates founded churches to serve their estates. They vary enormously in both acreage and in population. They could be geographically small, but densely populated city parishes, as in London or York, or large but sparsely populated and rural. Some large parishes were subdivided into townships, as in the case of Halifax in Yorkshire or Great Budworth in Cheshire. The parish church and minister would be central to both, however, and this often applied in a geographical as well as in an administrative and ecclesiastical sense. The parish was also expected to sustain its minister.

Parishes created a great many records over the centuries, some of which have survived, especially since the sixteenth and seventeenth centuries. Medieval records do exist, but are regrettably rare, though to be fair, far fewer were created (no parish registers, no poor law). Most of those for our period are now deposited in the appropriate county record office. The best introduction to parish records is W E Tate, *The Parish Chest* (3rd edn, 1969), which gives lots of examples of the types of parish records which exist. A useful book for ascertaining ancient parishes and their boundaries is the Phillimore Index to Parish Registers and www.genuki.org

Parish Registers

When genealogists refer to parish records, very often what are meant, to the exclusion of all else, are parish registers, and whilst these are not the only fruit of parochial administration, they are perhaps the single most important one. This is because they record almost everybody who was born, died and was married (even at times, Catholics, Nonconformists and Jews, especially where burials are concerned, because churchyards were the only place for the latter to take place). There is nothing which does likewise prior to parish registers. Researchers owe much to Thomas Cromwell, Henry VIII's chief minister in the 1530s. It was in 1538 that an Act was passed to instruct parishes to maintain and preserve parish registers of baptisms, marriages and burials. This was to prevent disputes about inheritance and to ascertain who was related to whom, and was part of the wider revolution in government initiated by the said Cromwell at this time.

Initially these registers were simply parchment books of blank pages (or loose sheets) in which all three forms of service were recorded. Entries are recorded as they occur, in date order, but divided into the three forms of service. In the case of baptisms, the baby's Christian name will appear first, then their parents' Christian name and surname. In the event of the few illegitimate births (about 1–3% of the total), the father's name often did not

Thomas Cromwell, originator of parish registers. Paul Lang's collection.

appear, and the term 'base born' will be used to signal disapproval. An amusing entry from the registers of St Mary's Hanwell is as follows, 'Thomas, son (daughter) of Thomas Messenger and Elizabeth his wife, was born and baptised October 24 1731, by the midwife, at the font, called a boy, and named by his godfather, Thomas, but proved a girl', but a more conventional one from the same register is that of 12 April 1789 of 'James Hughes, son of James and Hannah'. Baptisms, are of course not the same as births, but they usually occurred a few days, or at most a few weeks, after birth (infant mortality being very high); sometimes clergy recorded birth dates as well as baptism dates.

For marriages, the two parties will be named. At the parish of Sunbury on 15 April 1800 was recorded the marriage of John Banks and Jane Reynolds. It would usually be noted if one was from outside the parish. Thus, for the same parish on 12 May 1800, 'James Edwards of Reynoldstone, co. Glamorgan, and Sarah Lacy, lic[ence].' Occasionally occupation might be recorded as in the instance of John Saunders, carpenter, of Chertsey and Mary Watts, on 25 March 1722 at Sunbury. Most marrying are assumed to be bachelor and spinster, otherwise it will be noted as in this example, 'Benjamin Nurton, w[idower] and Martha Jackson, w[idow], both of St Saviour's, Southwark, lic[ence]'. For burials, simply the name of the deceased is recorded. A Hanwell example of 6 January 1788 simply notes 'Brown, James'. Sometimes there may be additional information, perhaps naming the husband of the deceased, or the parents if the death was of a child. An example of flesh being added to the skeleton was when John Slack of New Hutton was buried at Kendal on 16 December 1745 and it was noted that he had been 'kill'd by ye Scots', this being an incident on the retreat of the Jacobite rebels back to Scotland. Early registers have Christian names written in Latin.

Very few parishes have a complete set of registers dating back to 1538. Many of the earliest ones do not survive, written as they may have been on loose sheets of paper and poorly stored. Some clergy may have ignored the initial instructions from London. Religious upheaval caused by the radical Reformation and the conservative Catholic reaction of the 1550s did not help. By the end of the sixteenth century, most of the parish registers survive. There are often gaps during the Civil Wars and Commonwealth, 1642–60, when the regular minister was ejected by the Puritans and records were often ill kept or not at all.

In 1753 Lord Hardwicke's Marriage Act led to separate registers for marriages being created, though baptisms and burials were still recorded in the same book. It will usually be noted thereafter if the marriage was by licence, which as noted in the previous chapter was rare. Books recording banns of marriage also date from that time, due to the above Act being to prevent 'clandestine marriages'. Books recording banns, however, tend to survive less well than other registers.

The next major change was Rose's Act of 1812, which resulted in further regularization of parish registers, leading to more information being recorded there. Different books were now used for the different services, and they were laid out with forms denoting the information to be recorded. Baptism registers recorded date of baptism, Christian name of baby, surname of father and Christian names of both parents (father's name being omitted if unknown), father's profession and parish. On 19 March 1820 at Hanwell church, William, born on 31 December 1815, son of William and Harriett Taylor, labourer of Norwood, was baptized. Marriage registers recorded date, names and ages of both parties, with the husband's occupation. Thus at Hanwell, one example reads as follows, 'William Bishop of this parish, bachelor, and Jane Lewin of this parish, spinster, were married in the church by banns … this 21st day of November in the year 1819 … in the presence of Joseph Bishop and Fanny Bishop'. In the case of burials, the information is date, name and occupation of deceased. Another Hanwell example on 15 March 1834 was that of

Charlotte Obee of Ealing, Middlesex, aged 61. The minister who performed the service would sign his name, too.

If parish registers do not exist for the period in question, then all may not be lost. In 1598, bishop's (or parish) transcripts were introduced. The minister had to send to the bishop an annual copy of all the entries in the parish registers. I recall wanting to check whether Thomas Smethurst (a bigamist) really married Mary Durham in 1828 at St Mark's church, Kennington, but the parish registers were missing for that period. Fortunately the bishop's transcripts provided the answer (he was). Transcriptions can result in human errors, but where the originals no longer exist they are invaluable.

If you are fortunate, your ancestors may have been baptized, married or buried in a parish in which the Dade registers were in use. These were registers arranged to a pattern devised by the Revd William Dade. In the late eighteenth and early nineteenth centuries the dioceses of Chester and York used this system. They contain far more information than was usual prior to 1813 and also have information not used after that year, too. Baptism registers show, apart from the bare minimum, the child's seniority in the family, the father's occupation, the names, occupations and residences of the grandparents and the date of the infant's birth. Burial registers give the cause and date of death.

It will be highly unlikely that you will ever see an original parish register. Because parish registers were expected to be so popular, it was decided by county record offices to provide surrogates. Initially these were microfilmed and so are available thus. These can usually be viewed at the relevant county record office. Phillimore's *Atlas and Index to Parish Registers* lists their whereabouts, county by county, because county and diocesan boundaries have changed; some for the West Riding of Yorkshire are located at Nottinghamshire and Lancashire record offices as well as those in the West Riding itself.

All is not lost if you cannot visit the relevant repository. Some record offices may sell duplicate copies of microfilm of parish registers if they have the parish's permission to do so. There are other surrogate forms. Paper transcripts of some parish registers, chiefly marriage registers, were published in book form by Phillimore and by family history enthusiasts, sometimes indexed. Record societies have also published parish registers; the Thoresby Society did so for St Peter's church, Leeds. More recently some registers, especially those for London and Middlesex and West Yorkshire, have been digitized and so are available online at ancestry.co.uk. This makes searching easier, as many can be easily and quickly searched. There is also the International Genealogical Index, which is a vast index to baptisms and marriages only. It was originally available on microfiche but has been online for some years. However, the indexing is patchy; some parishes are covered for centuries, some for a few decades and some not at all. Just because a search is unsuccessful does not mean that the event did not occur, but that it may not be included in the IGI's coverage. Again, the Phillimore Index is an invaluable tool, because it lists the IGI's coverage for each parish. The Mormons have also constructed the British Vital Records Index, whose coverage is more extensive than the IGI.

Other relevant indexes are Pallot's Index of Marriages and Births, which covers most of the London and many of the Middlesex parishes from 1800–1837 (marriages), and 30,000 baptisms. It can be viewed on ancestry.co.uk. Boyd's Marriage Index covers many marriages which took place from 1538 to 1837, but the coverage is patchy. Registers from over 4,000 parishes were consulted, and there are 7 million names therein. The index is strong for East Anglia, however, and can be viewed online at Origins.net and on Findmypast.co.uk (the latter also has Boyd's London Burials, 1538–1872 and London miscellany, 1538–1775). Both the Society of Genealogists' Library and the Guildhall Library have copies, too, and the former has a vast collection of microfilmed parish registers. The Federation of Family History Societies are working on a National Burial Index, covering 1538 onwards and which has as its best coverage the early nineteenth century. This can be viewed on CD-Rom and on Findmypast.co.uk. Ancestry.co.uk also has a number of miscellaneous parish registers online.

A word about monumental inscriptions seen inside parish churches and the gravestones outside: these represent only a small proportion of those actually buried there. Most people in our period were too poor to be able to afford a stone tombstone, let alone a plaque inside the church. However if your ancestors were wealthy enough in order to do so, a visit to the church is certainly recommended. Memorials often give additional information about how an ancestor and his or her family wished them to be remembered, as their manifold virtues are listed therein. They may also give information about other family members. Many churches' inscriptions and gravestones have been transcribed and indexed by members of local family history societies, and these transcriptions are often available from the appropriate society and from the county or borough record office. Findmypast.co.uk has a searchable memorials index.

Two examples from St Mary's Acton give a flavour of these.

Near this Place
Lies the Body of
ELIZABETH BARRY
Of the Parish of St.
MARY SAVOY, who
Departed this life
Ye 7th of November 1713
Aged 55 years.

More informative is the following:

In the vault beneath are deposited the remains of
HARRIET
Third daughter of THOMAS and ELIZABETH SUSANNA
GRAHAM
And granddaughter of JOHN and ELIZABETH DAVENPORT
She died 30th September 1806
Aged 7 years
Also those of her father
THAMAS GRAHAM ESQRE
Of Edmond Castle Cumberland
And of CLAPHAM Common, Surrey
Who died 23rd June 1813
Aged 62 years
Also the remains of her mother
ELIZABETH SUSANNA GRAHAM
Relict of the above named THOMAS GRAHAM ESQRE
Who died in her house on Clapham Common
The 10th of August 1844, aged 81 years.

The Civil Parish

The parish had many other responsibilities, too, and of a secular nature, especially since the sixteenth century. The most important in terms of money and time was the administration of the Old Poor Law. Earlier legislation to deal with the poor was codified in 1601, replacing the older tradition of voluntary giving to the poor. The new law stated that each parish had to deal with its own poor. These were the people who were unable to support themselves, often due to extreme youth or old age, or infirmity. Unwed mothers with illegitimate children were also often in need. Men who were temporarily out of work due to illness were usually helped. The Act of Settlement of 1662 further defined the law. It stated that the parish only had to deal with those who were legally settled within its boundaries. To have settlement rights in any given parish, one either had to be born there, to have married someone who was born there, to have lived there without claiming relief for a year or to be occupying premises worth more than £10 per year. Those lacking such rights could be refused relief and sent on their way.

One important set of parish archives in this regard are the vestry minutes. The vestry was the parish's governing body, composed of the minister and the principal male residents of the parish. Readers of Jane Austen's *Emma* may recall references to Mr Knightley and Mr Weston attending parish meetings, but it was not confined to the gentry.

*Parish chest, repository of parish records, St Martin's, West Drayton,
Middlesex, 2010.* Author.

Shopkeepers, such as East Hoathley's Thomas Turner, and farmers also
attended. From among these would be the parish officers,
churchwarden(s), overseers, surveyor of the highways and constable
(sometimes known as headborough and formerly an officer of the manor).
These officials were appointed annually, usually at Easter, were unpaid
and amateur. They made important decisions at the meetings held
throughout the year, often monthly. They had to decide how much money
should be levied in the way of rates (see Chapter 10) and how it should be
spent. The vestry was responsible for the relief of the local poor, the upkeep
of local roads and bridges and the maintenance of the church fabric. These
parish officers were answerable to the JPs(justices of the peace) at quarter
sessions, and the latter had to settle disputes between the parishes, which
usually concerned poor relief.

These important decisions were recorded in vestry minute books and
other sources. Vestry minutes record the date of each meeting, with a list
of those who attended, so if your ancestor was among the parish elite you
can trace how long he was in the parish by when he is first and last listed
here. They may include nothing else but total annual expenditure and
income. Some, though, are far more informative. They list the decisions
that were made. These often refer to other parishioners by name. Those in
need of relief may be mentioned, and the reasons for relief may well be

given, such as sickness, unemployment or old age. Orphans might be apprenticed to a master, as was the fictional Oliver Twist. An example from the Hanwell Vestry Minutes of 2 April 1827 records the names of three vestrymen at the meeting, plus the overseer, his deputy and a church-warden. At the meeting, 'Mrs Talbot applied for some clothing for her daughter, who was gone out to service. Agreed that the mother and child meet Mr Berry [the deputy overseer] at Brentford tomorrow or as soon as convenient to be provided with necessaries for the said purpose.'

The parish officers, as listed above, were important local figures. The most hard-working, at least in theory, were the overseers, because they had to deal face to face with the local poor. All these officials kept accounts books, and some survive, mostly those of churchwardens and overseers. These give a good indication of what these officials actually did. These often allude to the people to whom poor relief was paid. There could be lists of parishioners in claim of relief. Often there were people who received a regular income from the parish, and these were listed in the overseers' disbursement books. Then there were those who received one-off payments to tide them over a temporary crisis. These payments were considered to be outdoor relief. They were often in money, but not always so. Payments could be in kind, including the provision of food, clothing and fuel. Sometimes travellers might be relieved, such as soldiers and sailors returning home, or pregnant women. The latter were especially important to move on, because if they gave birth in the parish, they would acquire legal settlement and so be a burden on the rates. However these people are rarely named and accounts merely refer to giving money to travelling strangers.

For the parish of Norwood, there are lists of widows who received a regular pension. In 1653 it was noted, 'Item payd to the widow Bland from the 27th day of February to the 25th day of March 0-8-0 [8s]'. Six other widows were also listed (surnames only) and the sums paid to them, four shillings only. In 1680, the overseers recorded they paid tradesmen various sums for goods required. Mr Room received 2s 5½d 'for cloaths' and Thomas Beaton had two shillings 'for making two coats and waistcoats'.

In 1834 the New Poor Law led to the workhouse system; this was known as indoor relief, though this was far from universal. As this is mostly after our period, it does not need to be considered here. However, legislation passed in the eighteenth century, notably the Workhouse Act of 1722, did enable parishes to build poor houses in which paupers were accommo-dated and fed in return for work, though these were usually small. Parishes could also club together and have one such building to serve several parishes. By about 1750, there were 600 workhouses, housing about 30,000 people in all. Private Acts of Parliament could also lead to workhouses being built. Lists of inmates may survive, giving dates of admission and discharge, and reason for entry.

There were also certificates of settlement, which date from 1697. These were pieces of paper signed by the parish officers which were given to someone who had settlement rights in the parish but who went elsewhere to work. They stated that, if they (and any accompanying dependants) fell on hard times and needed relief, the parish of origin would accept them back (or pay for their relief in their new parish) and that the parish where

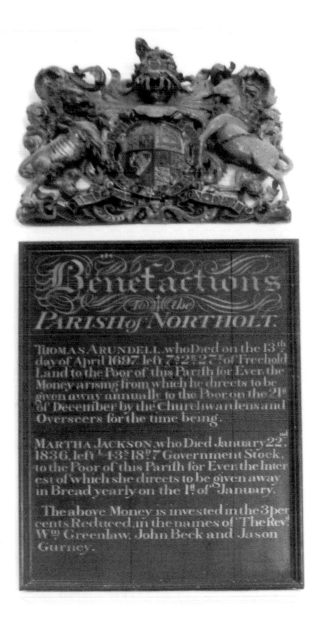

Charity notice board, St Mary's, Northolt, Middlesex, 2010. Author.

they had moved to would not have them as a burden to the rates. Usually overseers looked on potentially poor strangers with hostility and often quickly sent them elsewhere.

Bastardy was another issue for the parish officers. They had to discover who the father was and make him responsible for the child's upkeep, in order to reduce the burden on rates. A bond would be entered into whereby the father would agree to pay for his child, if he could not be persuaded to marry the mother. Alternatively he could pay a lump sum to the parish in order to discharge all responsibility. Parish records often include reference to such practices and bastardy bonds survive.

It is important to note that many of a parish's poor are not recorded in these documents. Many survived with the help of friends, family and neighbours. Some resorted to petty theft. Private charity helped some. Not all were assisted by the parish. Even where records do survive, they may only list parish officers, attendees at meetings and total expenditure and income, rather than listing payments and recipients. Bastardy might result in a private financial agreement which went unrecorded in parish records.

Apprentices have already been mentioned. Children who were orphaned were sometimes apprenticed, either to another parishioner or outside the parish, often prior to the usual age of apprenticeship, which was 14 years. This was in order to remove the child from the parish's responsibility and so ease the burden on the rates. Vestry minutes and apprenticeship indentures should give details of child and master, the latter's trade, the date and the sum of money given to the new master. They should also detail other conditions in the agreement between parish and master. Complaints about the ill treatment of children were sometimes discussed in vestry minutes.

Constables, churchwardens and surveyors of the highways also kept account books, but their survival is less extensive. It seems that church-wardens' accounts are more likely to exist from before the eighteenth century in the south of England, and that constables' accounts survive least well of all the parish officers. These accounts rarely mention individuals, except of course those who held that particular office in any one year. If your ancestor was a parish officer, you will find an insight into his duties in these books, assuming of course that they are itemized, which is not always the case.

The churchwardens were the senior officers, and were responsible for the upkeep of the church fabric. Repairs of the building and any other expense concerning the place were their duty. They also paid the bell ringers to ring on auspicious dates, such as royal anniversaries or military victories. Surveyors were to oversee repairs to parish roads and bridges and the constable dealt with evildoers. His duties also included taking prisoners to the county gaol or attending trials, searching the parish for vagrants and, in times of war and rebellion, supplying men or arms for the militia.

All this expenditure was financed by rates levied on the parishioners and these will be discussed be Chapter 10.

Miscellaneous Parish Records

Apart from the main classes of records, there are many miscellaneous ones which appear among some parish archives. Charity records are one such. Wealthy parishioners often left money in their wills to buy land or stock and then to have the interest used to feed, clothe or educate the local poor. The clergyman and vestry often administered these charities; names of the charitable can often be seen on boards in the church, detailing the bequests. However it is relatively unusual for lists of recipients to have been made. There may be copies of the censuses of 1801–31 which were compiled by the parish officers, and are dealt with in Chapter 11. There may be legal records concerning disputes which the parish entered into, perhaps over tithes or charities. Papers concerning disagreements with other parishes over settlement might exist. Deeds and charters may survive. There may even be medieval documents. Lists of pew rents may also exist: names of wealthy parishioners who paid fees for the best pews. As with much in archival research, looking through the catalogues of deposited archives, whether online or in paper form, can be a useful exercise, if documents can be located which cover, or might cover, the time span that your ancestors were residing in the parish. Some parishes were very good at preserving their archives, but this is not always the case. It is certainly worth looking beyond parish registers, and looking at other material, too. All these will be found at the appropriate county or borough record office; some have been microfilmed but most have not, so you will be able to view centuries-old documents.

Nonconformists and Catholics

Although by the seventeenth century the vast majority of the population were Anglican, it is worth noting that not all were. After the Act of Supremacy in 1559, Catholics and members of various forms of Protestant Dissent became marginalized and at times subject to fines, imprisonment and discrimination, which declined after 1689 for Nonconformists but only in the late eighteenth century for Catholics. Despite this, Catholicism remained relatively strong in Lancashire, Northumberland, Hampshire and London, but there were also pockets throughout the country. Nonconformists were more numerous, and especially so in the South-West, the eastern counties, Yorkshire, and London. As stated, they will often be recorded in burial registers, but their chapels created their own archives, too.

Surviving Nonconformist registers of baptisms, marriages and deaths up until 1837 are often held at TNA. Unlike Anglican registers, the baptism registers note the mother's maiden name. They can be searched for online under 'Select More Records and Documents' and then choose 'Non-Conformist registers', and these can be searched for by name. There are a few registers of pre-1837 Catholic churches at TNA, though most are for the north of England (RG 4) We should remember that Anglican registers often recorded the baptisms, marriages and burials of Nonconformists and Catholics, too, especially for marriages, 1754–1837. Online Nonconformist registers can also be seen at bmdregisters.com and indexes are at Familysearch/IGI. Most Catholic registers date from 1791, when practising the religion was no longer penalized; most of the registers are still with the churches, but some have been deposited and the Catholic Record Society has published some (available at TNA and elsewhere).

Parish registers are one of the most important records for genealogy for the period 1538–1837, because almost everyone will be recorded here somewhere and sometime. But it must be stressed that parish registers are not the only fruit of the parish. Poor law records are also important, as are other records which once lay in the parish chest and which are now mostly in county record offices.

Chapter 4

THE PROFESSIONALS

It is easiest of all to trace your ancestor's career if he belonged to one of the professions, because archives of former members and their career progression are readily available. Most people worked on the land before the mid-nineteenth century (as agricultural labourers), whilst others engaged in trade, industry, crafts or were in domestic service (especially women), and for the majority of these, no records survive. Yet others followed a profession – the church, the law, medicine being ancient ones, but increasingly the state became an important employer too, especially from the later seventeenth century. State employees also were part of the armed forces, the civil service and enforcing law and order. Major business corporations included the East India Company and the older livery companies and these kept archives. Many of these professions required their entrants to be educated at school and university, though education was for a minority, especially higher education.

University Records

For clergymen, a university degree was compulsory, but many other boys would have attended one of the colleges of Oxford or Cambridge from the Middle Ages to the present, too. There are a number of published registers of students, which are arranged alphabetically and give a short biography, including dates of matriculation and any degrees awarded, future career, birth and death dates, where born and perhaps father's name. Try J and J A Venn, *Alumni Cantabrigienses* for Cambridge and A B Emden, *Biographical Register of the University of Oxford*, for the thirteenth century to 1540, and J Foster, *Alumni Oxonienses* for 1500–1886. Most graduates until the nineteenth century went on to enter the Church, law or medicine. There are also registers for individual colleges, too, and *The Times* online lists names of those who graduated. Of course, others attended other universities, including those in Scotland and Leyden, in the Netherlands, in the eighteenth century. Such books often refer to a pupil's subsequent career, so if he went on to be a clergyman, it would list the benefices he held, with dates. Catholics were barred from British universities from the

St John's College, Oxford, 1920s. Author's collection.

Reformation until the nineteenth century, so Catholic youths often went abroad, to France or Spain, for their education.

Schools

Education was not compulsory until 1880 and the state did not sponsor schooling in any form until 1833. However there were a great number of private schools. Many were very small and left no record, save for adverts in the local press and entries in directories. Even well-established ones, with some renown – the Great Ealing School was attended, amongst others, by W S Gilbert, John Henry Newman and Thomas Huxley, for instance – failed to leave any corpus of records. The records of former private schools, where they exist, tend to be in local authority archives. For schools which still survive, records may remain in situ.

Then there are the great public schools, such as Eton, Harrow, Westminster and Winchester, and for boys attending these, research is usually straightforward. A researcher should first check that there are published lists of former pupils – as there are for Harrow and Westminster from the eighteenth century. These can be found on the open shelves of TNA library for instance and should always be consulted prior to contacting a particular school. Many published lists of alumni are to be found at the Society of Genealogists' Library, too, along with school histories. These lists are arranged in chronological order, and there is usually an index. They give details of home and parents, school career (dates of entry and discharge) and subsequent career details and (perhaps) death.

There were also special schools aimed at particular groups. Lewisham Archives have the records of the Congregational School, for sons of Congregational ministers, and the Royal Naval School, for sons of naval officers. Archives of grammar schools and charity schools may also exist. These may also include lists of pupils.

The Inns of Chancery and of Court

Although civil law was taught at Oxford and Cambridge from the Middle Ages, they did not teach common law until the mid-nineteenth century. Any youth wanting to be a solicitor could attend a number of Inns of Chancery in London from the Middle Ages until their extinction in the nineteenth century. These were preparatory schools for lawyers. Unfortunately pupil lists for only four of at least a dozen have survived. Records survive at TNA for Clement's Inn and the Library of the Middle Temple for New Inn. The Law Society (Staple Inn) and those for Barnard's Inn were published by the Selden Society in 1995.

Would-be barristers had to spend seven to eight years at one of the Inns of Court (until the 1840s), these four being Gray's Inn, Lincoln's Inn, the Middle Temple and the Inner Temple. Numbers too increased, with 230 barristers practising in 1780. Admission registers exist for all four inns. Many have been published and so are relatively easily available, Middle Temple (1501–1975), Inner Temple (1547–1850, available on a database); Gray's Inn (1521–1889) and Lincoln's Inn (1420–1893). All these courts have libraries which have much other information, as well as that already mentioned. Lawyers will be discussed further in Chapter 7.

These registers often detail pupils' fathers, too, with name and occupation.

The Apprenticeship System

Apart from schools and colleges, there was another once common method of educating youths of both sexes, which was particularly prevalent in the seventeenth and eighteenth centuries. This was the system of apprenticeship. A master of a trade was paid to take a youth to serve under him in order that the young man would learn the business on the job. He would enter into a formal contract with his master, usually when aged 14, but possibly as young as 12, and would normally serve seven years. He would work in return for pocket money and board and lodgings. The lot of apprentices varied considerably, as Hogarth's painting of the idle and the industrious apprentices shows – the former ends up on the gallows, the second ends up marrying his master's daughter.

This system began following the Statute of Apprentices of 1563, which forbade anyone from entering a trade who had not served the said apprenticeship. This legislation remained in force, with modifications, until 1814. Stamp duty was payable on the indentures of apprenticeship from 1710. These survive in the form of apprenticeship books and are held at TNA (IR 1) and must be seen on microfilm. These include lists of articled clerks. They are arranged geographically (for London see the 'City' registers, and 'Country' registers for the rest of the country), and then roughly chronologically. They list the name, address and trade of the master, the name of the apprentice and the date of the indenture. Sometimes the names of the apprentice's parents are also given. There are indexes for the years 1710–74. However the tax was not collected until a few years after the apprenticeship was completed.

Some apprentices enlisted in the armed forces, contrary to the terms of their apprenticeship indentures, and once this was discovered, they were returned to their masters. Lists of these youths for 1806–35 can be found in TNA, WO 25/2962. There were also military and naval apprenticeships, for boys from the Royal Naval Asylum at Greenwich and at the Duke of York's Military School, Chelsea (often sons of former sailors or soldiers, many were orphans). They can be found in TNA, WO 143/52, covering 1806–48 and in ADM 73/421–48, covering 1808–38, respectively. There were also apprenticeships in the Merchant Navy from 1823 too. For London, these can be found in TNA, BT 150/1–14 (covering 1824–79). These give details of the apprentice's name, age, date, terms of apprenticeship and his master's name.

The Watermen and Lightermen's Company were responsible for traffic on the Thames from the sixteenth to the twentieth century and many of their employees were previously apprentices. The Guildhall Library has the apprentice binding books for 1688–1908 (MS 6289) and the apprentice affidavit books, 1759–1897 (MS 6291). These give the apprentice's name, the date and place of baptism, the date he began his apprenticeship and the date he became a free waterman, as well as naming his master, who may be his father – occasionally his mother, if the father was deceased.

Many apprenticeships were exempt from the stamp duty already mentioned and so do not appear in the registers above. These would include children apprenticed by charities or by parish vestries or if those apprenticed to their father. Vestry minute books refer to children of poor parents, or orphans, whom the parish paid to have apprenticed so they would no longer be a burden on the parish rates. There may be additional references to the apprentice if there was trouble – Hanwell Vestry investigated a case where it was alleged that a master had ill used his apprentice and steps were taken against the master to try and ensure it would not recur. One charity which paid to apprentice children was Thomas Coram's Foundling Hospital. The London Metropolitan Archives (LMA) has registers of apprentices which are accessible for 1751–1891 (A/FH/A12/003/001–3). These are indexed alphabetically. JPs also authorized the apprenticeships of poor children; minutes of the Blackheath JPs are to be found at the Greenwich History Centre.

Apprentices sometimes found themselves in trouble with the law. The Middlesex Quarter Sessions refers to apprentices in dispute with their masters. Pepys makes reference in the later 1660s to apprentices being involved in riots; and they were said to be prominent in the anti-Catholic rioting in London in 1688. It may be worth checking criminal records, if your ancestor was an apprentice, therefore. It should also be noted that it is estimated that about half of those who began apprenticeships in London failed to complete them.

Some apprenticeship records are online, at Origins.net (London apprenticeship abstracts, 1442–1850) and at Findmypast.co.uk (apprenticeship records, 1710–74).

The Church, Law and Medicine

Doctors, lawyers and clergymen are all easy to track down in published sources other than those already mentioned. The *Law List*, has names from 1775 onwards. We should also note G Hennessey's *Novum Repertorum Ecclesiasticum Parochiale Londinense*, covering London clergy from 1321 to 1898, and which is indexed. They are organized in alphabetical order by surname, though often within subsections – medical listings in the nineteenth century are divided into two sections – 'London' and 'Country', whereas the *Law Lists* have different sections for barristers, London solicitors and provincial lawyers. They give the age, address, educational and career history of the professional; retired members are also included. When names cease to appear, they are probably dead.

Once you have traced your ancestor by these lists, it may be sensible to carry on looking through the series of these volumes as far as you can in both directions, learning more information (and seeing much of the same, too) as you proceed. Significant runs of these volumes can be found at the LMA, TNA and the Guildhall Library.

Directories will also list these people, perhaps in both the 'Court' and 'Business' sections. They are more likely to have obituaries (for dates of death see burial registers or wills) in the local press as they are often significant figures in the local community. Newspapers carried adverts for private schools, giving details of the curriculum, fees, when the school was established and so on. Clergymen were often schoolmasters, too; in the

Priest, Holy Cross Church, Greenford, Middlesex. 2010 Author.

eighteenth century, the Revd William Dodd ran a boys' school in Ealing as well as being a royal chaplain (and a forger).

There are other sources. For clergy, ordination papers for the diocese are often held at county record offices, and the ongoing clergymen's database (www.kcl.ac.uk/humanities/cch/cce/), aiming to cover all Anglican clergy for 1536–1834, may also be worth a look and is expanding constantly. Many of the professions are listed in directories, too, and lawyers should appear in records of trials.

Business Records

It is always easier to learn about the man at the top than his clerks and labourers. Senior figures in the business world are usually allotted obituary columns in the local and sometimes national press. But what about the majority of employees? Tracking them down is often a matter of luck. Some business archives do survive, but many tend to be account books, minutes of board meetings, advertising material, product details and so forth, all of which help give an impression about the company, but may say little about employees – as with school log books.

Some local authority archives have excellent holdings of business archives. However, staff records only survive for a very few firms.

Businesses often took out insurance on their property and goods. Several insurance firms sprang up in the later seventeenth century, partly as a response to the Great Fire of 1666. Their archives can provide useful information about businesses, although they also covered domestic property. In some cases, of course, the business was run from the owner's house. The information given in the following sets of registers usually includes the number of the policy, the name/location of the agent, name, status, occupation and address of the policy holder, location of the premises, type and nature of the property, its value, the premium paid and when the renewal was due. Details of any tenants might also be given, if applicable. Fire policy registers exist for the Hand-in-Hand insurance company for 1696–1865 (Ms 8674-8, 166 vols), the Sun, 1710–1863 (Ms 11936–7, 1262 vols) and the Royal Exchange, 1753–9 and 1773–1883 (Ms 7252–5, 173 vols). All are held at the Guildhall Library. If these huge numbers of registers arranged chronologically sound daunting, do bear in mind that there are a number of indexes. There is an online name index for the Sun for 1800–39. When researching a book about Richmond murders in 2009, I was pleased to discover that in March 1834 Thomas Smethurst (who was tried for the murder of his bigamous wife in 1859) took out a policy with the Sun on his apothecary's business in south London – although he was not to qualify as an apothecary until some months later! There is also a card index at the LMA for the Sun's policies for 1714–31 (Ms 17817) and a microfiche index to both Sun and Royal Exchange policies for 1775–87 (Ms 24172). Those for that other major London insurer, the Phoenix, are located at Cambridge University Library.

The City of London Livery Companies

In the Middle Ages, a number of livery companies were formed in the City, eventually numbering over 100, and encompassing numerous trades and professions, including leather sellers, apothecaries and booksellers, to name but three. These companies had extensive powers over the individual trades which they represented. They could fix prices, working conditions and regulate the quality of goods for sale. They could also prohibit trade by non-members and undertook the training of apprentices. Once a man became a Freeman of the Company he could legitimately set up shop in the City. In fact, trading in the City was prohibited unless a man was a member of one of these companies, though he did not necessarily have to be of the Company in which he was trading. In order to become a Freeman, a man had to either undertake several years of apprenticeship, or his father had to be a member of the Company (through patrimony), or rarest of all, through redemption, a man could buy his way in. However, as the centuries passed, the role of the companies altered and they became more and more involved in charitable undertakings and education: the Stationers' Company founding the Stationers' School in Hornsey in the nineteenth century for example. Most still survive to this day and are involved in such roles.

Records of Freemen and apprentices exist for most of these companies, dating from the Middle Ages to the twentieth century. Those for the Grocers' Company date from 1345–1652 and 1686–1952 for membership, and for apprentices from 1457–1505 and 1629–1933, for example. Those for London are available at the LMA on microfilm. These records can give the name, date of birth and address of the apprentice, and perhaps his father's details, plus details of whom he was apprenticed with and for how long. For the Apothecaries' Company, for example, there are registers of the Court of Examiners, for the apprentices had to take examinations (after 1815). These tell which apothecaries the apprentices worked under, the hospitals they worked in and which subjects they were taught. It then states when they were examined and whether they passed or not. Since apprentices had to be successful in all counts, some had to retake examinations a number of times. However, some companies have not deposited their records at the LMA, such as the Leather Sellers, and anyone interested in these should contact the Clerk of the Company in the first instance.

It should be noted that the membership of these livery companies was low, and decreased as the proportion of the men in London engaged on that particular undertaking decreased as time went on. If, for example, your ancestor was working as a leather seller near St Paul's Cathedral in the early eighteenth century, it is highly likely that he was a member of the Company in question. However, if your ancestor was engaged in the same trade in, say, Bermondsey in the following century, it is highly unlikely that he would have been a member. The archivist to the Company informed the author that he receives many enquiries from those with London ancestors involved in the leather trade whom they imagine must have been members of the Company, but has to inform them that this was not the case.

Politicians

It is relatively easy to learn about MPs from official publications, especially the HMSO House of Commons volumes, available in all good libraries, covering the Middle Ages to the nineteenth century, listing MPs alphabetically and providing a brief biography of each. Newspapers also refer to candidates prior to elections when they use the press to solicit the electorate's votes.

Many more men were involved in local government. In my career, I am frequently asked by researchers who are convinced that their ancestor was a former mayor to produce lists of mayors of all the local authorities

Geoffrey Chaucer, royal servant and poet. Paul Lang's collection.

covered by the present borough. Some researchers are quickly disillu-sioned to learn that their ancestor was a councillor but never mayor. Many will appear in corporation minute books, found in borough or county record offices.

Local newspapers are another good source for the history of councillors and would-be councillors, especially towards the end of our period. In the lead-up to any local election, there will usually be brief biographies of each candidate, and what they stood for, as well as which party they repre-sented. Election addresses and results will tell you how successful they were, and these, together with obituaries of local politicians are regular staples of the local press.

Civil Servants

As the seat of central government from the eleventh century, most of the government's employees have worked in London, and as the scope of governmental activities increased in the seventeenth and eighteenth centuries, their number has soared. However, the survival of records concerning individual civil servants is patchy.

As ever, it is easier to find out about those who held senior grades. *The British Imperial Calendar*, from 1809 to 1972, listed those at senior grades, with name, rank and department and educational achievements. Earlier civil servants can be located in *The Royal Kalendar*, 1767–1890. Incomplete series can be found at TNA.

Details of officials from 1557 to 1745 may be found in the *Calendars of Treasury Papers* and *Treasury Books*, which are published and indexed. Civil Service Evidence of Age records for 1752–1948 can be seen online at Findmypast.co.uk.

The Army

Britain did not possess a standing army until 1660, and although England has been involved in numerous conflicts at home and abroad from earliest times to the emergence of the Tudors, we know little of them. However, there are a number of sources which may be worth investigating for the Middle Ages. The first concerns those who came over with William the Conqueror. The best source for these is A J Camp's book, *My Ancestors Came over with the Conqueror* (1988). Very few people, of course, can trace their ancestors this far back, and usually only through a female line. A list of some of those who fought on Henry V's side at Agincourt in 1415 can be found in *The History of the Battle of Agincourt . . . the Roll of the Men at Arms* (1827). Thousands of men who fought in the Hundred Years War (1337–1453) are listed at www.medievalsoldier.org. Names of gentry and nobility present at the battle of Bosworth can be found in M Bennett, *The*

Battle of Bosworth (2000). Finally, there may be other military muster rolls taken in counties in the Middle Ages, and now possibly located at county record offices. They may list, parish by parish, some at least, of those able-bodied men of the county, along with their weapons, who were eligible for military service. Whether they did see active service, against either the French or the Scots, is unknown, but these lists could be a useful tool, especially if you had an ancestor in that parish in this period. Expect them to be written, of course, in Latin.

The most serious conflict in English history was the Civil Wars of 1642–51, which cumulatively killed proportionately more Britons than the First World War: at least 100,000 of a population of perhaps about 4 million. However, we know more about those who were officers than the majority of men who served in the ranks. For example, there are published lists of men who officered regiments on both sides during the Civil Wars, and these have been published in various books (C Firth and G Davies, *The Regimental History of Cromwell's Army* (1940) and S Reid's *Officers and Regiments of the Royalist Army* (4 vols, 1985–8)). Those on the war's losing side suffered, and there is much about them and their finances in two indexed calendars at TNA: *Calendar of the Proceedings of the Committee for Advance of Money, 1642–1656* and *Calendar of the Proceedings of the Committee for Compounding . . . 1643–1660*.

After the Civil Wars were over and Cromwell was triumphant, substantial armed forces were maintained. This was unusual in peacetime, but since his power derived from the army it could hardly be otherwise. When

Fifteenth-century knights' arms and armour. Paul Lang's collection.

the monarchy was restored in 1660, the army was reduced in size, but was maintained as a useful adjunct to civil power. With Britain becoming a great power by the beginning of the eighteenth century, the numbers in the regular army increased.

As ever it is easier to trace officers. There are published lists of officers for Queen Anne's reign, Charles Dalton's *George I's Army* and the army list for 1740. From 1754 there is the annually produced *Army List*. All these publications list officers by unit, and give a brief account of their service history. All are indexed. There is also an indexed list to officers from 1702–52 at TNA, WO64. For the rank and file, you will need to know in which unit he served, or be prepared to spend much time researching. Regimental pay and muster rolls from 1732–1878 exist in WO12, and description books for 1756–1900 in WO25.

Some men, having left the army, were granted pensions and lived at the Chelsea Hospital, founded in 1691. Soldiers' Documents for pensioners can be found at TNA, WO97 (1760–1913). These give name, age, birthplace, trade prior to enlistment, service record and reason for discharge. Disability pension records can be found, in date order, for 1715–1882 at TNA, WO116/1–124. Other discharge documents covering 1782–1833 are at WO121/137–22. Muster Rolls (1702–1865) and admissions books (1778–1917) can be found at TNA, WO23. Registers of baptisms (1691–1812), marriages (1691–1765) and burials (1692–1856) are also at TNA, RG4/4330–2 and 4387. Men discharged from 1760 to 1854 can be searched for on TNA's online catalogue. Deserters are occasionally listed in the marching order books, at TNA in series WO5.

Officers and men of the regiments of Guards are to be found at the Guards' Museum in London. Records of cavalrymen from 1799–1919 are at TNA.

Soldiers who served at Waterloo can be found online at ancestry.co.uk, which has the Waterloo Medal Roll (37,000 names), and the medal roll for soldiers, 1793–1949. For details of about 9,000 soldiers serving in the Peninsular War of 1807–14, try napoleon-series.org. Rolls of other soldiers from 1656–1888 are on Origins.net, as are births, marriages and deaths of soldiers from the late eighteenth to the twentieth centuries.

Records of the militia and volunteer forces are dealt with in Chapter 11.

The Royal Navy

As with the army, few personal records survive prior to the Restoration. Ships' muster books survive from 1667, and these list sailors. They are located at TNA, ADM36. More detailed records commence in 1764, when men's age and birthplace are given. Ships' pay books also list sailors. As always, tracing officers is easier, with the quarterly *Navy List* from 1814.

The National Maritime Museum has a typescript listing all naval officers from 1660–1815. The 28,000 men who served at Trafalgar can be searched for on a database, www.nationalarchives.gov.uk/trafalgarancestors. Ancestry.co.uk has a roll of naval officers from 1660–1815.

There is little information about Merchant Navy men prior to 1835, but the LMA has a list of petitions from 8,000 of them and their families from 1787–1854, or they can be searched for on www.originsnetwork.com. Muster rolls of seamen post-1747 are to be found at the Maritime History Archive at Newfoundland University on www.mun.ca/mha/holdings/crewlist.php.

The Royal Household

Monarchs have employed many people in their households. The Royal Archives holds a card index for those employed in the Lord Chamberlain's and Lord Stewards' from 1660–1837, and there are lists by Sainty and Burcholz in *Officials of the Royal Household, 1660–1837*. TNA has a number of archives pertaining to royal servants' appointments and payments on series LC3 and LC5. Garden and kitchen staff are in series LS. Records for the household prior to 1660 are generally fewer, but for 1523–1696 some are listed separately in tax records, E179.

East India Company

This joint stock company was incorporated in 1660 and established trading posts in India. It also maintained its own armed forces. Its archives are at the British Library and include records of births, marriages and burials of its employees in India. From 1803 printed lists of all its employees were published annually, and these survive. They also have lists of Company ships' surgeons and ship log books list particulars of men punished.

The Police

Apart from the railway police, the Metropolitan Police Force was Britain's first police force, founded by Sir Robert Peel in 1829, and is the largest one in terms of personnel, budget and in renown. Originally there were but 3,000 men, who patrolled central London.

The archives for its personnel are to be found at TNA, because it was originally under the control of the Home Secretary, so was part of central government's records (county forces were under the control of the county magistrates, then the county councillors, and so are often held in county record offices).

There are various sources of information about members of the force. Probably the best method is to begin by using the alphabetical list of men who joined, which covers 1830–57, which has been microfilmed (MEPO 4/333–8). This will give rank, division, dates of appointment and removal, and also the warrant number, which is a key reference for further research.

If the ancestor might have died in service between 1829 and 1889, check MEPO 4/2, which is indexed and gives the cause of death. For the first few thousands of recruits, HO 65/26 is an alphabetical register, 1829–1836. Early recruits from 1829–30 can be located in MEPO 4/31–2, arranged by warrant number. These give the officer's height and why he was dismissed (often due to drinking on duty). There are also a number of name indexes, compiled using these records, and which are available at TNA.

Before the Metropolitan Police were introduced into outer London parishes, many had their own watch forces, and records often survive of personnel. Lewisham Archives have documents listing their special constables for 1830–2. TNA holds records of the Bow Street Runners, the force predating the Met. Horse Patrol records are in MEPO2/25; for the men of the Foot Patrol, see MEPO4/508. Provincial police forces did not exist until after the 1839 Police Act, so need not concern us here. However, towns often employed watchmen, sometimes discharged servicemen, and urban magistrates' records may mention the names of men employed on such duties.

Readers will note that these professionals noted are always referred to as 'he'. This is because there was relatively little scope for working women in these professions until the late nineteenth century at the very earliest.

Chapter 5

THE COURTS, PART 1: CRIMINAL

M any of our ancestors have been involved in crime, either as victim, perpetrator, suspect, juror or magistrate. Many courts have existed in the past which dealt with crime, and they have imposed different types of punishment. These courts have created a vast corpus of archives which can be examined by researchers. It is worth pointing out that, up to 1733, Latin was the language of legal record, and we will revisit this in Appendix 1. However, this rule was not always prevalent, and in any case the key parts of documents can usually be understood without one having to be able to translate their entirety.

Assizes

The assize courts were introduced in Henry II's reign throughout England. They divided the country into six circuits, each of several adjoining counties: the northern, the Midlands, Oxford, Home, Western and Norfolk. There were also the palatine jurisdictions of Cheshire, Durham and Lancashire, which, although they were outside these circuits, operated in a similar manner. Middlesex, which included London, was also outside the six circuits and was under the jurisdiction of the Central Criminal Court, popularly known as the Old Bailey.

Assize judges toured each circuit twice a year to try criminals at the county town. They tried capital offences; not only murder, but many others, and there was no firm dividing line between those tried at the assizes and those tried at quarter sessions, since, for example, both courts could try theft and assault.

Assize records post-1559 are held at TNA in series ASSI. They include lists of judges, jurors and those accused. Indictment files lay out the charge against the prisoner, but list the latter as having a fictitious occupation and parish of origin (this will almost always be where the offence took place instead). Deposition files, giving witness statements, are a more reliable guide to details about a prisoner. To take an example from the Northern Assizes of summer 1749. Thomas Mawson, a black drummer in a regiment

Execution of the Earl of Stafford, 1641.
Paul Lang's collection.

of dragoons, killed John Johnson, an officer's servant. Mawson is described (fictitiously)as being 'a yeoman'. Apparently, according to one witness, the latter 'did make an assault ... did strike and push the said John Johnson with his hands and knees in and upon the left side of the belly of him'. Mawson's statement was that Johnson was a friend of his previously, but instigated the quarrel that led to his death. Dr Cotes was another witness and he deposed that Johnson was already in a poor state of health prior to the brawl. Mawson was acquitted.

Gaol and minute books often list the accused, in chronological order, and summarize cases, noting plea, verdict and sentence. Few records survive for the Middle Ages (to be found at JUST1, 3, 4 and at KB9); from the sixteenth century their survival is more common, but even then it can be patchy and varies between counties. For example, for Bedfordshire, there is an almost complete run of indictments from 1658, but there are no surviving depositions prior to 1832. A useful list, county by county, of surviving archives post-sixteenth century, is given in *Family History at TNA*. They do not include transcripts of trials, giving what was actually said. Newspaper accounts are a useful source for this, but are fairly limited until the nineteenth century unless the case was of unusual interest, such as in the case of the mysterious death of a Cambridge undergraduate in 1746.

Some assize records have been indexed in the Calendar of Assize Records, which covers those of the Home Circuit (Essex, Kent, Hertfordshire, Surrey and Sussex) for the sixteenth and seventeenth centuries. Witnesses at the North Eastern Circuit between 1613 and 1800 can be found in the catalogue for ASSI 45. However, most are unindexed, so if you do not know when a trial took place, or indeed if you have crim inal ancestors at all, searching these records could be a very time-consuming business indeed.

Middlesex/London was outside the assize system, and was covered by the Central Criminal Court, the Old Bailey. For the period 1674–1913, transcripts of the trials have been made available at www.oldbailey.online. Furthermore these can be searched by the names of anyone listed in the transcripts, including witnesses, places and types of offence. Well worth a speculative search.

Another important London criminal court was the King's Bench, although it also heard trials from elsewhere in Britain. Plea rolls are KB26–8 and for indictment files KB9, up to 1675, then divided into London cases (KB10) and elsewhere (KB11). Witness statements survive in KB1–2, especially from the eighteenth century onwards. There is a contemporary index to plea rolls at IND1; for London and Middlesex this is for 1673–1843, 1638–1704 and 1765–1843.

The palatinate jurisdictions of Chester, Lancashire and Durham are to be found at TNA, in, respectively, CHES, PL and DURH. These assize records are very similar to those already mentioned.

The Court Leet

This was a manorial court which dealt with petty offences and will be detailed further in Chapter 9. However it is worth noting that in some counties it continued to administer justice until the seventeenth century when it was superseded by the quarter sessions.

Quarter Sessions

Justice was also administered on a county basis (Yorkshire, having three ridings, had three; some boroughs also had their own court, too). It was in 1285 that the office of Justice of the Peace (JP) was first introduced. A JP was a magistrate, unpaid and always a man of local substance, as the office carried a property qualification. He could pass judgment in person by himself on minor offences, or with one or two colleagues, in what was known as petty sessions, though these only begin to be formally recorded by the early nineteenth century. All the county's JPs would meet together four times a year in a prominent town in the county; hence their meetings were known as quarter sessions, which commenced in 1361.

JPs could deal with a vast number of offences, including theft, sedition, witchcraft, assault, disturbance of the peace and keeping an unlicensed alehouse. Theft could be a capital offence, depending on the value of the goods stolen (goods worth over a shilling were classified as being grand larceny and carried a capital sentence), some being deliberately under-valued. From the sixteenth century, they were also given social and economic legislation to implement and administer, especially concerning the welfare of the poor and the upkeep of bridges and roads. They also had to deal with religious dissidents: Catholics and Protestant Nonconformists. From the sixteenth to the nineteenth centuries the JPs were the real rulers of the counties, so had immense power.

Many archives were created by the actions of quarter sessions, though most only survive from the sixteenth century onwards. Perhaps the principal records are the Order Books, also known as Minute Books. These are the official records of the four annual meetings of the court. They usually begin with the date and place of the meeting, then list those magistrates present. There then should be a list of decisions of the court. Those accused of crimes, with brief details of offence and location, are listed, then the sentence is recorded. Indictment bills are another major source. They are often grouped together by the date of the sessions which dealt with them. These are scraps of paper, each one concerning a different defendant, with his or her age, parish and occupation. The crime will be stated and, if it is a theft, the value of the item stolen is often given. At the end there will be the note 'true bill' if the defendant was found guilty. There may also be lists of prisoners and witnesses. Periodically those not attending their Anglican church would be fined, so lists of those fined, with occupation and address are given, though after about 1689 this feature of quarter sessions died out as Nonconformists were legally allowed to worship.

These records also show judgments when the JPs were called to arbitrate between parishes in dispute with one another. It was not unknown for parishes to squabble over who should pay poor relief for a pauper whose settlement was uncertain. The JPs would decide between the parishes and allocate responsibility accordingly.

These archives are to be found at the county record office to which the archives relate (those few surviving records for the fourteenth and fifteenth centuries are at TNA, JUST 1). As said, their survival is variable and there may be gaps, especially with the earlier centuries. In some cases you will be allowed to view the original documents. Elsewhere, such as at Cheshire Archives and the Centre for Kentish Studies, the documents will be on microfilm.

Some corporations, such as York and Newcastle, also had the power to hold criminal courts, and their records are similar to those of the county quarter sessions. These records will be found in the borough archives of the city in question.

Some quarter sessions records have been indexed and published, and this is obviously a very great help. These include Middlesex (Westminster was excluded from the county's jurisdiction, up to 1844) for 1559–1709, Hertfordshire and the North Riding of Yorkshire, all in several volumes. So even if you don't know whether your ancestors were caught up in crime, but you know that they lived in these counties in the periods covered by these, a speculative search is always worthwhile and relatively quick.

Punishments

There were a number of sentences which could be imposed on those found guilty. Mutilation, flogging, hanging (beheading was for the nobility only) and, later, transportation, were four of the better known. The basic punishment should be noted in the assize or quarter sessions archives.

Transportation was first introduced in 1615 as an alternative to the death sentence. Prisoners had to petition for mercy and would be shipped out to the American colonies, where they would be sent to work on the plantations. From 1718, this would usually be for seven years if the offence was non-capital and fourteen if it was a capital sentence. The number transported from 1615 to 1775 was about 40,000. As well as criminals, after unsuccessful rebellions against the Crown in 1685, 1715 and 1745, many hundreds were sent to the colonies for given periods of time, but many never returned.

With the onset of rebellion in the colonies in 1775, this practice could not be continued and prisoners were held in hulks for a period. Yet with the discovery of Australia in the next decade, there was a new home for convicts. Transportation was at its height in the 1830s, with an average of 4,000 transportees per year. After our period the number rapidly declined, especially after the Penal Servitude Act of 1853 and in 1867 transportation to Australia ended. Between 1787 and 1867, over 160,000 people were sent to Australia this way.

The stocks, Aldbury, Surrey. Paul Lang's collection.

Transportation records are available at TNA. Those sent to the West Indies or the American colonies can be searched for on CD-Rom, *British Emigrants in Bondage*, covering 48,000 people from 1614–1788. This gives a convict's name, the date and place of the trial, occupation, month and year of departure and arrival, name of the ship and destination. *Treasury Books* (T53) for 1716–44 list convicts from the Home Counties, the ship they sailed on, the captain's name and destination. *Calendars of State Papers Colonial America and West Indies* provide similar information, up to 1734. Transportation records can also be seen on Ancestry.

Those sent to Australia are recorded by date of transportation and then by county where sentence was passed. They will name the ship sailed on, date of departure and arrival, and destination. Transportation did not always occur immediately after the trial; it could take up to a year or two later. Details can be viewed on microfilm at HO11, but the ones for Australia have been published and indexed in numerous volumes. They can also be seen in TNA's library. They give prisoner's name, name of the ship they sailed on, date of despatch and arrival and the name of the province they arrived at. You should also learn when they gained their parole.

Musters were taken in Australia between 1788 and 1867 and these can identify what happened to convicts after arrival (series HO10). Names, age, religion, residence, occupation, family, land held and whether they arrived as free emigrants or convicts are all noted.

Prisons

Although we now think of incarceration as the principal method of punishment, except for community service, this was a Victorian concept. Until the nineteenth century, prisons were primarily to hold prisoners prior to trial and prior to receiving their actual punishment. Prisons were rarely purpose-built structures, but often converted buildings, such as castles, as in the case of Guildford in Surrey and Lancaster Castle. There were also village lock ups, usually capable of holding one or two prisoners for a very temporary time period. There were also houses of correction, such as that in Wakefield. Those who were in prison for any length of time were usually debtors, and we'll investigate this in the next chapter. For most of the period covered by this book, it was the county's High Sheriff who was responsible for the county gaol and also for entertaining the assize judges on their bi-annual visit.

Calendars of gaol delivery list prisoners in any one prison at particular times. These are usually held in the record office for the county where that gaol was located. Some prison records are still held at the prison itself, but these tend to be the more recent ones, so few researchers pre-1837 will need to contact them.

Some registers of prisoners are held at TNA. These are returns for Middlesex and London for 1792–1849, held in series HO26. For the rest of England and Wales, HO27 includes returns from gaol registers from 1805.

Some prisoners were held in prison hulks, old ships which were often

Interior of the Tower of London. Paul Lang's collection.

moored near Royal Navy establishments. These were in use from 1776 to 1857 and usually were temporary holding stages for prisoners awaiting transportation. This was especially the case in 1776–87 in the hiatus when there was nowhere for them to be sent (the American colonies being in revolt and Australia being as yet undiscovered). Registers of prisoners in hulks are held at TNA, series HO9, for the years 1802–49. Quarterly registers of prisoners in hulks from 1824 are held at HO8. These can give information about the behaviour and health of the prisoners, when they left the ships and/or were transferred to other gaols. Quarterly returns also exist for 1802–31 at T38/310–38. Indexes to a few particular ships have also survived, at ADM6/418–23 and HO7/3, covering the 1820s and 1830s.

Appeals for Mercy and Pardons

Many crimes carried the death penalty, but its execution (no pun intended) was relatively rare. In part this was because there were petitions for mercy sent on the behalf of the condemned. Youth, extreme old age, provocation, dependent relatives and previous good character were all used to advocate a lesser punishment. These are found at TNA. Patent Rolls (series C66) from 1654–1717 include pardons on condition of transportation, but detail is minimal and these records are in Latin. Prior to 1784, the Secretaries of State were written to, so a search of State Papers Domestic is often required. Criminal Entry Books in SP44 are another useful source for pardons, refusals and respites in the eighteenth century.

From 1782, the Home Office correspondence in HO42 can be checked, but so great was the volume of work in this regard that a separate record series was created, HO47, covering 1784–1830. These are judges' reports following the end of assizes and Old Bailey sessions in which capital verdicts had been given. They give the judges' opinions on the verdict and the jurors and witnesses. There can be character references concerning the accused and other personal information about them. Some of these reports have been indexed (the first twenty-two volumes covering 1783–99) and work is ongoing and has currently reached the early 1830s. Outcomes of petitions can be found in the Criminal Entry Books in series HO13, and the above indexes include references to these books, too. Other letters and statements from trial judges from 1819–40 are in series HO6 and these can give further information about the condemned and their crimes. Actual petitions for mercy from 1819–40 can be located at HO17, and these are being indexed, too. Formal records of pardons from 1782–1849 are in HO13.

Treason

'Treason ne'er doth prosper/What's the reason?/Because if treason prosper/None dare call it treason' ran a sixteenth-century ditty. Rebellion against the English and from 1707 British state rarely succeeded. Those who ended up on the losing side often paid the penalty with their life or liberty. Major rebellions, such as those in 1685 (Monmouth's rebellion) and the two major Jacobite rebellions (1715 and 1745) resulted in large numbers of prisoners. Special commissions of judges were appointed by the government to try these prisoners. Only a small proportion were executed; most were transported, some were pardoned, a few escaped, some were pardoned on enlistment in the army and some died in prison. The fates of some are unknown, so presumably they died in prison. Sedition was a lesser offence; those speaking in public against the monarch or saluting their foes could earn a fine, gaol sentence or a whipping. Both quarter sessions and assizes dealt with such offences.

Wigfield's *The Monmouth Rebels* (1985) provides lists of those transported following this rebellion. Lists of the several hundreds of English Jacobite prisoners of 1715 and their fates can be found in Gooch's *The Desperate Faction* (1995), for the north-east of England and for the north-west in Oates's *Last Battle on English Soil* (forthcoming). Those far fewer English prisoners of 1745 can be found in the *Scottish Historical Series* 'Prisoners of the 45' (1928–9). All are arranged alphabetically and evidence has been taken from a variety of archives at TNA, especially KB8/66 for 1715, and TS11 for 1745. The latter include brief statements of the evidence against each man, and reasons they gave to minimize their guilt (for example, inebriation on enlistment). State Papers Domestic also list prisoners. These records can give the name, occupation, parish of origin, unit in which the man served, rank, prison career as well as eventual fate, but not all this information is available for each man.

Other Sources

Don't forget that newspapers, especially towards the end of our period, carried detailed reports of crime, especially murder. Where there was a crime but no one was brought to trial, they can be the only source; thus for the unsolved highway murder of Samuel Verry in Ealing in 1747, the only existing accounts feature in *The General Advertiser* of 1747. Metropolitan police records can also detail criminal investigations, though only for the very end of our period. The murder of Eliza Davis in north London in 1837 is covered in TNA, MEPO3/41. These sources will deal with the crimes which never reached court because no one was ever charged with them. The murder just cited was never solved, for instance.

Sheriffs' papers concerning costs of imprisonment and execution can be located at E370 (1714–1832), T64 (1745–85), T90 (1733–1822) and at T207 (1823–59). Newspapers and broadsheets (a single page of information about a certain topic) often reported executions and included dying speeches (often spurious). Comments on the sympathies of the crowd are noted, because up to 1868 all executions were in public, so provided a popular spectacle. It was alleged that when the Revd William Dodd was hanged at Tyburn for forgery in 1777 half a million turned out to line the route and to see the sight. He addressed the audience, 'which words were uttered with so moving and unaffected, emphasis, as to draw tears, apparently, from eyes unused to weep, men, women and children of all ranks, were observed to weep, a genuine evidence of gentle hearts and unutterable anguish'.

Published sources can be useful for a relatively small number of particularly notorious crimes. *The Newgate Calendar*, published in numerous volumes (now available online), provided lurid or moralizing accounts of ferocious crimes carried out by highwaymen, sadistic mistresses and evil footpads.

We should recall that others were involved in the criminal courts, too, not just those accused. There were the magistrates, law officers, witnesses and victims. The magistrates at quarter sessions were the JPs. They were not necessarily men with any legal training, and usually were not, but they were the gentry of the counties, the propertied elite. Most were well educated and many had been to university, so registers of private and public schools, as well as university registers, as noted in Chapter 4, should carry some relevant details. Collectively a county's JPs were known as the Commission of the Peace. They were chosen from lists supplied to the Secretaries of State by the county's Lord Lieutenant. Many did not always attend quarter sessions, but those that did should be listed in the official records of those sessions meetings. By the later eighteenth century there were an increasing number of clergymen among their ranks. The assize judges were professional lawyers and have been discussed in Chapter 4.

Until 1829 there was no professional police force in England. Those responsible for bringing miscreants before the courts were either the parish constables, or the High Constables, or, especially around London, the Bow Street Runners. These men were a relatively small force, initially numbering a mere six men, but expanded as the eighteenth century progressed and divided into mounted and foot patrols. Records for the former can be found in TNA, MEPO2/25. A service register, unindexed, for the foot patrols, covering 1821–9, is at TNA, MEPO4/508. It gives name, address, age, place of birth, height, marital status, number of children, name of recommender, military service and date of appointment, and date and reason for discharge. In 1835 the Horse Patrol was merged with the Met; the foot patrol in 1839. The Metropolitan Police have been described in Chapter 4.

Witnesses often appear in court records, where they can be identified together with occupation and address. However they are difficult to locate, unindexed as they are, except in rare cases, among deposition files. Even so, many of these files have been heavily weeded, so may no longer exist.

Jurors are often listed in assize papers. They were taken from a locality's male population. Court records rarely say much about the victim of crime except for a very brief description of name, occupation and address.

Other useful indexes include *British Trials, 1660–1900* (only a small minority of the whole), on microfiche and searchable by defendant, victim and location; *Summary Convictions in Wiltshire*, on a searchable CD-Rom, and covering 1698–1903: 26,500 convictions. Ancestors caught up in the Swing Riots in southern England in 1830–2 might turn up in the *Swing Unmasked* CD, which has 3,300 names. *Kent at Law* is an index to Kent wrongdoers in 1602.

Most people will have an ancestor who has been caught up in the criminal system at one point in their lives. There are numerous possible sources to turn to. Some are indexed and so the routes to them are straightforward. Otherwise, you will need an approximate date, and then have to check which sources survive, and investigate them.

Chapter 6

THE COURTS, PART 2: CIVIL

It was not just the criminal law which has had an impact on our ancestors' lives, though that is certainly better known. Many people have recourse to the law by choice, over land, property and money, in dispute with a second party. There were numerous courts, mostly now long defunct, which dealt with different aspects of civil law and we shall now explore them and the archives they created. The archives below, unless stated otherwise, are held at TNA. Manorial courts are dealt with in Chapter 9.

Medieval England developed a system of common law, unlike the Continent or Scotland, which derived from the unwritten customs of the country. They were used by the Court of Common Pleas, King's Bench and Chancery. However, this system could not enforce judgments. Equity courts, such as the equity part of the Chancery Court and the Exchequer, could do so. The two systems of justice coexisted until 1841.

Courts were divided not by type of case but by type of plaintiff. Thus King's Bench dealt with actions between the Crown and its subjects, Exchequer with litigation between Crown debtors and Common Pleas between the Crown's subjects.

Chancery

The Court of Chancery, overseen by the Lord Chancellor, was used by many people between the fourteenth and nineteenth centuries. They did so in order to settle disputes over inheritance, land, trusts, debts, apprenticeships and marriage settlements. These proceedings resulted in the creation of masses of documentation, still relatively little used by researchers.

Those wishing to settle grievances were known as the plaintiff and would approach a lawyer for him to draw up a bill of complaint against the party they believed had wronged them, known as the defendant. This would give the plaintiff's name, address, occupation and the cause of complaint. The defendant would then make a written reply to the points raised and this could result in rejoinders. Finally, a list of the points at law would emerge. Evidence was then gathered together to be examined by the court's officers. Of course the dispute might well be settled out of court, in which case the documentation would cease.

If this was not the case, then an agreed number of deponents would be examined under oath with a number of agreed questions. The answers (depositions) would be recorded and these should say a lot about the parties involved as well as about the case itself. They will also give information about the deponents, too. Finally, the court would make its decision and these are recorded in Entry Books of Decrees and Orders. There are contemporary annual indexes for 1546–1875.

For the early centuries of the court's existence, names appearing in pleadings before the court can be found by an online search of TNA's catalogue. For class C6, Equity Pleas, 1625–1714, a name search will give a catalogue reference to a document with a case involving that name and so that can be seen at TNA. However, for the period 1558–1625 there is as yet no online catalogue, although there are a number of paper catalogues and indexes available at TNA, covering these years. Another source, this time to deponents, the Bernau indexes (1558–1714 for country cases and 1534–1853 for town cases), is available at the Society of Genealogists' Library. This index also covers pleadings from 1715–58. The difficulty with this index is that it gives obsolete TNA references, but these should be copied and kept for translation into current numbering, which should be possible at TNA. Most of the records created were written in English, too, even before 1733.

Exchequer Equity Court Proceedings

This court was established in the sixteenth century and became the second Exchequer Court (the other being the Exchequer Court of Pleas). It dealt with cases involving land, and rights pertaining to land, such as tithes, debts and wills, where the plaintiff could allege, usually factiously, that the Crown had an interest. Horowitz's *Exchequer Equity Records and Proceedings, 1649–1841* is the specialist guide to these records. Since the depositions in E134 are searchable online, these will bring you into a law suit in which your ancestor was involved as plaintiff, defendant or subject in dispute. Deponents are excluded from this index, but from 1559–1695 can be found in unindexed lists at TNA and the Society of Genealogists' Library.

One of the main classes of records produced were Bills. These were created by the plaintiff and set out the case against the defendant. They also give brief personal details of both parties. Bills from 1558–1841 are at E112, and the best way into these is by using the indexes to defendants and plaintiffs, IND1/16820–53, which are divided by reign. Records listing whether the defendant appeared in court are to be found in E107 and in Memoranda Rolls in E193.

Following the Bills were the depositions, where witnesses were examined. Those taken in London from 1558–1841 are in E133 and can be searched online by defendant or plaintiff. Depositions taken by Commission in the country for the same dates are at E134. There may be additional information in E103 among the affidavits from 1774–1841.

The Court of Star Chamber

This court had a sinister reputation, which probably originated from its use by James I and Charles I against their political enemies, and so became unpopular with Parliament, and it was abolished in 1641. It had been instituted in 1485 and met in the Palace of Westminster to enforce law and order. It also handled private disputes about property rights. One case occurred in 1530 when the Rector of Hayes, the Revd Thomas Gold, brought it against his parishioners whom he claimed were denying him his full tithe income. Unfortunately, although we know much about the grievances of the parties, there is nothing to state the outcome of the case.

Many of the case files (STAC1–8) survive and can be searched for online by name. These detail the proceedings in the court, and these are, unusually, in English. However, not all the records survive. The decree and order books, which list the court's decisions, do not, so the outcome of cases is unknown. Star Chamber proceedings can also be read in various record society publications covering cases in Somerset, Sussex and Yorkshire.

The Court of Requests

This was founded by Richard III in 1483 and Ricardians (those people who are enthusiasts of the king) also refer to it as proof that the wicked king of legend was really good King Richard. It was to enable the poor to have access to royal justice. Cases handled included title to property, annuities, villeinage, forgery, perjury and marriage contracts. Records survive in far more quantity than for the Star Chamber, with the majority of order and decree books still existing, for example. Records are held in REQ1 and 2. The court records cease to exist in 1642.

The Court of Augmentations

This was an administrative court as well as a court of law, set up in 1536 to deal with the transfer of land from the Crown from the monasteries following their dissolution in that year. It dealt with disputes over land, rights claimed by monastic tenants and others owed money by the monasteries. Surviving records include pleadings (E321), depositions and decrees (both E315) for the entirety of its existence. The court was absorbed by the Exchequer Court in 1554. Manuscript indexes exist to plaintiffs and defendants in pleadings and depositions, but not decrees.

The Court of Wards

This court existed from 1540 to 1649 and handled disputes over widows' remarriage, sale of wardships of children and the insane, and fines for leases of wards' lands. Pleadings, decrees, depositions and evidences, among other records, exist in class WARD1–15. However, many of these are unfit for production as they are damaged, nor are there any finding aids.

The Palatinate Courts

Chester, Lancashire and Durham were all palatinate jurisdictions from the fifteenth to the nineteenth centuries, so fell outside the remit of the civil courts previously listed. All possessed their own equity courts. However not all are equally accessible as the availability of finding aids and indexes varies. If you are looking for a case in Chester (CHES), paper indexes exist for 1509–58 (for series CHES15/1) and for 1760–1820 (for CHES 15/156–78) for the plaintiffs' names in the pleadings. Although the first list only has 194 names, the second has almost 5,000. Decrees and depositions are not indexed, but exist, so if you have a date from the pleadings, these other record series could be checked by date.

The records for Durham's courts (DURH) exist in an equal quantity, but have not been indexed, making them more time-consuming to use. Work is taking place on Lancashire courts, on indexing of pleadings (PL6 and 7) and depositions (PL10).

The Duchy of Lancaster Court

Not to be confused with the palatinate court mentioned above, the duchy was created in the fourteenth century. It owned land throughout the country and tenants were able to use its court in the Savoy in London. Pleadings from 1485–1603 have been indexed in three volumes known as *Ducatus Lancastriae*. For later years, from 1603–1832, try the manuscript indexes at IND1/6918–22.

High Court of the Admiralty

As the name suggests, this court dealt with maritime matters, but it was a civil court unconnected with the Royal Navy. Cases concerning commercial disputes including salvage rights, lost cargoes and damage to ships were the principal business of the court. If your ancestors were ship owners or were involved in seaborne trade in other ways, then the archives created by these courts could be of interest to you. They are held at TNA, and there are two main classes of records. First there are the examinations and answers in HCA13, covering 1531–1768. These are all in English. They give the name, residence, age and occupation of the witnesses who gave evidence at the court. An index exists at IND1/10322. Then there are the instance papers in HCA15–18, covering 1586–1874. These include affidavits, answers, petitions, decrees, allegations and exhibits. There are also indexes to ships' names at HCA56, for 1772–1946.

High Court of Delegates

Established in the early sixteenth century, it was not abolished until 1833. It heard appeals from the ecclesiastical courts, each of which required the appointment of a special commission of judges delegate appointed by the Lord Chancellor. Proceedings are to be found in TNA, DEL1–2.

Debtors

Imprisonment for debt was common prior to 1868 and debtors were the most common prisoners, numbering thousands in the eighteenth and nineteenth centuries. Anyone owing over £100 up to 1842 was declared a bankrupt. Courts would take the debtors' property and distribute it to the creditors, which could prevent a debtor being gaoled. Bankrupts and insolvent debtors are usually listed in *The London Gazette*, from 1684 and 1712 respectively, which gives a little detail: name, address, occupation and sometimes names and details of creditors. Conviction and imprisonment

Lincoln Castle, once home to debtors. Paul Lang's collection.

might also be mentioned. These also appear in *The Times* online (1785–1985).

Prison records can be found at the appropriate county record office. A few London ones are held at TNA. These include those of the Palace Court, 1630–1849, which specialized in holding Westminster debtors, found at PALA1–9. The Fleet, King's Bench, Marshalsea and the Queen's prison records of 1685–1862 are at PRIS1–11. Registers for Lincoln Gaol, 1810–22, PCOM2/309 are also, oddly enough, held at TNA.

There were also Acts passed to relieve debtors, allowing them to petition a JP for release from gaol. Quarter session records at county record offices may include these. Those for the palatine of Chester from 1760–1830 are held at TNA, CHES10. In 1813 the Court for the Relief of Insolvent Debtors was formed. Petitions for relief from 1813–62 are registered at TNA, B6/45–71 and indexed at B8. A small number of bankruptcy files also exist for the period after 1759 in TNA, B3, with most dating between 1780 and 1842. Another source are the registers of commissions of bankruptcy, 1710–1849, in B4, giving name and address of bankrupt, with names of creditors or solicitor acting for the bankrupt. Indexed registers of certificates of Conformity also name bankrupts, with addresses, for 1733–1817, at TNA, B6. Other papers for 1710–1846 survive at B5.

Petitions

Individuals and groups petitioned the monarch for a particular favour. Those created from the thirteenth to the early seventeenth century can be viewed online at TNA's website and can be searched by name. They are particularly numerous in the fourteenth century. Most were sent by the middling people and the wealthy, though some are from villeins.

Plea Rolls

Actions brought under common law in the courts of the Exchequer, Common Pleas and King's Bench can be found, up to 1482, in *A Calendar of Pleas and Memoranda Rolls*.

Civil Court cases can also be found in the press, especially in *The Times*, and these can be searched for online at The Times digital archive. This can be a useful entry point into the archives of the legal system. Another good entry point is to try an online search on TNA's catalogue for Equity Pleadings.

Chapter 7

PUBLISHED SOURCES
AND LISTS

The printing press had come into being in England in the later fifteenth century, but was little used at first. By the eighteenth century, literacy was becoming more the norm for some in society. Urban-dwelling men were more likely to be able to read than their rural counterparts and women. They helped to generate a demand for the written word, and the published word became more common in that century. Even when people were not literate, they usually knew someone who was who could read to his friends and neighbours, perhaps in a public place such as an inn, and published matter often went through several hands.

Newspapers

Although there were newspapers of a kind during the Civil Wars of the 1640s, these were primarily propaganda sheets and in any case ran for fairly short runs. The first long-standing newspaper was *The Oxford Gazette*, later *The London Gazette*, in 1665. Other newspapers appeared and, with the ending of official censorship in 1695, many more appeared. Most were two or four pages long. Some were thrice-weekly such as the fore-mentioned *Gazette*, and some were weekly. The first daily was *The Daily Courant* in 1702. Until 1712, these newspapers were all published in London. The first regional newspaper was *The Newcastle Courant*, followed a few years later by *The Leeds Mercury*. By the mid-eighteenth century there were few major provincial towns or cities, certainly not in the north of England and the Midlands, which did not have their own newspaper; some had two or three. Towns in the south-east of England, being so near to London, were rather slower to publish their own, save for *The Kentish Post*, based in Canterbury. Most were weekly. None was published on a Sunday until 1822. There were also monthly magazines, such as *The Political State of Great Britain*, 1711–40, and better known, *The Gentleman's Magazine*, first published in 1731 and which continued until 1868. TNA has sets of these and the latter are available at the British Library, too, as well as many other institutions, and online on ancestry.com.

Newspapers, then as now, carried national, foreign and local news. They covered war and political controversy. There was financial and shipping news. Crime was a feature. Here is one example:

> Last Tuesday, John Franklyn, John Cochis and Annie Hipson were committed to Salisbury Gaol, for counterfeiting the coin of this kingdom, several pieces of false coin and tools being found upon them, diligent search is making after several others.

They also carried advertisements and personal news of deaths and marriages. To give two examples, taken from *The General Advertiser* of 1746:

> Yesterday was married, at St. Paul's, Mr Ambrose, an eminent attorney in Bishopsgate Street, to a Miss Clark, Daughter of Mr Clark of Gray's in Kent, a beautiful young lady with a considerable fortune.

A few Days since died at his living of Aston Clinton in Bucks; the Rev. Dr Waldo, minister of that place, aged 75; about a fortnight before his death, apprehending his Approaching Dissolution, he preach'd his farewell sermon to his congregation, which was so moving and pathetic; as drew Tears from his Auditors, he was possess'd of a very good Temporal Estate; which he has left to his eldest son, Mr Waldo, a career in Newgate Street. *The Gentleman's Magazine* included national and foreign news, archaeological finds, book reviews, poetry and politics. For our purposes, the two main sections are probably 'Domestic Occurrences' and the Births, Marriages and Deaths sections. The former includes accounts of unusual deaths and accidents. In November 1807 we learn of a fire at Mr Bentley's warehouse on Fleet Street, London, and of the death, by disease, of Mr Summerfield's 2½-year-old son in Westminster. The births are mostly those of the offspring of gentry, nobility, clergy, merchants and officers, and likewise for marriages. Deaths are rather more substantial, with obituaries often included. These include humbler folk. For instance, on 25 September 1807:

> Accidentally shot, Andrew James Bazell, a corporal. He was the non commissioned officer of a small detachment of soldiers for escorting three deserters to the depot in the Isle of Wight. While the party was refreshing themselves at a little public house between Ashford and Hampton, Anson, one of the privates, was laying down his arms and accoutrements, when the piece suddenly went off, and lodged its contents in Bazell's body, below his right arm, which caused his instant death. The deceased and Anson were particularly good friends.

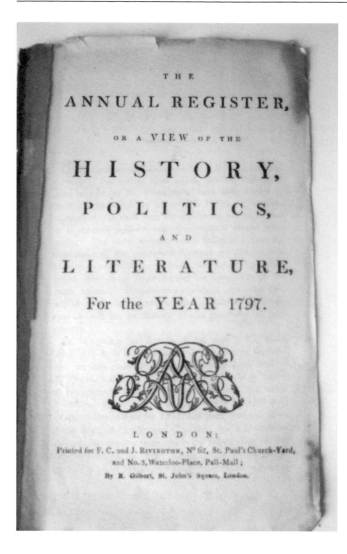

The Annual Register, *1797*. Author's collection.

A similar publication was *The Annual Register*, first published in 1758 and still in publication at the time of writing. However, as its name suggested, it was annual, unlike the monthly *Gentleman's Magazine*. It did, as ever, include births (parents' names and sex of baby, with date), marriages and deaths of the better off in society. Promotions in the armed forces and church are also listed, though selectively. In its 'Domestic Occurrences', it lists news, often including violent deaths and murderous attacks. However it is not well indexed and includes a great deal of foreign news. It can be seen at TNA and some libraries.

In 1785 *The Times* was first published, and this has the advantage that it can be searched online. Initially it was four pages long and was published daily, Sundays excepted. It carried far more detail than the newspapers of the earlier part of the century. Property adverts were a major feature and often detail the contents of the house, listing furniture and objects therein. As ever, births, deaths and marriages were included. Trials of criminals were given in far more detail than had been the case hitherto. Civil cases were often printed on the front page, with cases before the Court of Common Pleas and the Court of King's Bench. Again, these were detailed, though not verbatim, accounts of the cases heard in court, with synopses of evidence and legal arguments. Bankrupts are listed, though briefly, as in the following example from 1829, 'Joseph William Coe, Bath, silk mercer, June 18, 19, July 17th at the Bankrupts' Court, Basinghall Street, solicitors Messrs Stokes and Hollingsworth, Cateston Street'.

Local newspapers carried as much international and national news as other periodicals, with very little local news. What little there was was contained in a section headed 'Country News', meaning news of events outside London. Newspapers often cut and pasted news from other newspapers to include in theirs. They were often only two or four pages long, with almost no pictures. Advertisements, then as now, take up much of each newspaper. These are often for property, listing the seller, but also for other goods. Sometimes theatrical performances are advertised, giving company members. Bankruptcies are listed. So too are women who have fled their husbands, with the latter stating that they will be no longer responsible for their departed spouse's debts!

The best single source, though far from comprehensive for the local press, for newspapers in the UK is the British Library Newspaper Library at Colindale, a short walk from the tube station. Some of the newspapers have been microfilmed but many are still available in paper format. These newspapers are listed on their website, so you can determine what they have and for which dates (it is possible to search by title and place). The British Library itself at St Pancras holds a fine collection of national newspapers from 1625–1800, all of which is microfilmed. The Bodleian Library also has collections of local newspapers, too. County libraries usually have their county newspaper to be viewed; Oxford Central Library's local studies room has the *Oxford and Reading Gazette* to view, and Newcastle's City Library has copies of the three Newcastle newspapers from the early eighteenth century onwards. Not all early copies of these newspapers survive. There are very few editions of *The Newcastle Courant* from 1712 (the year of its founding) to 1718. There are no known copies of *The Leeds Mercury* from 1745–9.

The great difficulty with using these is that so few have been indexed, however, and few newspapers, have been digitized prior to 1800 (*The Times* being the exception). A small number of nineteenth-century newspapers, both national and local, have been digitized and so can be searched with

British Library Newspaper Library, Colindale, 2011. Author's collection.

ease. These can be viewed for free at institutions which have subscribed to the site, otherwise payment is necessary. Ancestry.co.uk has Andrew's newspaper index cards (1790–1976), which include many references to births, marriages and obituaries.

Indexes of newspapers are few and far between, but as always, it is worth enquiring if an index has been created by volunteers or staff. Most only cover a few years, however, and they are not always complete. An exception is *The Gentleman's Magazine*, for which there is an index for obituaries and biographies from 1731–80 and for marriages, 1731–68. Each volume is also indexed, for names. The first twenty volumes are available online at ancestry.com. The British Library has had forty-nine nineteenth-century newspapers digitalized, so these can be searched online (www.nineteenthcenturynewspapers/bl/), and of these, thirty-five cover the years prior to 1837. This is a subscription site and so fees must be paid for searches, but some institutions and libraries do subscribe to it, allowing their readers to search for free.

It should be stressed that, unlike newspapers in the twentieth century and beyond, most of the births, marriages and deaths recorded are of those of the nobility, gentry and clergy. If your ancestor was an army officer who was killed or wounded in battle he may well have been given an honourable mention; but the rank and file are not named therein. Poorer people's deaths tend to be published only if there was something unusual about them; perhaps a fatal accident, murder, suicide or extreme (and often spurious) longevity. However, people from the middling ranks might be included in county newspapers. For example, *The Sussex Weekly Advertiser* for 11 February 1793 noted 'last Thursday, died, at East Hoathley, Mr Thomas Turner, many years a shop keeper at that place', yet the death of John Lucas, a Leeds teacher and antiquarian, did not merit a reference in *The Leeds Mercury* in 1750.

Lists of people might also be published in newspapers if they were involved in a particular activity. *The London Gazette* listed in 1745 those who attended the Archbishop of York's meeting at York when he preached against the danger posed by the Jacobite rebellion of that year. The same newspaper also listed those merchants who supported the government at this time by accepting notes as well as coinage. After the rebellion was over, *The York Journal* listed, parish by parish, all those in the city (about 2,000 names are listed) who had subscribed to the paying of forces raised against the Jacobites, together with the sums paid and noting a small number of defaulters.

Directories

Readers will be familiar with telephone directories. Directories of another kind, though essentially the same, have existed since the seventeenth century. The first-known English directory was published in 1638 for London; there was not another until 1677; and then not until the next century, but after 1734 they were more regular. However, by the later eighteenth century, major provincial cities, such as Liverpool, began to publish them. Some volumes covered several counties. *The Universal British Directory* (published in the 1790s), a work of several volumes, covered the whole country. One well-known firm of directory publishers in the early nineteenth century was *Pigot's*, from 1814–53, and they also aimed at national coverage.

At first, directories were listings of merchants in the city, in alphabetical order, with their address and type of business. Later they tend to list nobility, gentry and clergy (known as the 'principal inhabitants'), shopkeepers and publicans, though for villages they will be organized by village, no address being given. They may be organized alphabetically or by type of trade.

These are of immense importance for anyone whose ancestor was in business in the seventeenth to the nineteenth century; though only a minority of towns and cities are included until the late eighteenth century. For the majority of people who were not in trade or were among the nobility, gentry or clergy, there will be no mention of them whatsoever. Labourers and domestic servants are unremarked upon.

Let us illustrate this with an example taken from *Pigot's Directory* for

Middlesex for 1832. It is divided roughly by parish, in alphabetical order, though in some cases some small parishes are lumped together with their neighbours. So, for Isleworth, which had, in 1831, a population of 5,590, we learn about this village 'delightfully situated on the northern bank of the Thames', the key businesses, the churches and local charities. Then there is a list of the nobility, gentry and clergy, numbering fifty-one, including such notables as the Duke of Northumberland of Syon House and the Earl of Jersey of Osterley Park. There are women, too, in the list, albeit in a minority and never being graced with Christian names, such as Mrs Thompson on Gumley Row and Miss Golding of Church Street. Then there are about 150 others, including schoolmasters, market gardeners, publicans and shopkeepers of many descriptions, divided by trade. Again, although there are a few female names, such as Mary Pyke and Elizabeth Rance, milliners both, these are in a very small minority (under 5%). About 4–5% of the village's inhabitants are listed, but with an average household of five, the directory has listed about one-fifth of its householders.

Directories can be found in county libraries, county and borough record offices. The best collection, however, is at the Guildhall Library, where there are directories from across the country. Most directories are in paper format. Some have been digitized. A small number from 1750–1919 were digitized by a project based at Leicester University, www.historicaldirectories.org/hd/. Some others can be found at www.Genuki.org.uk.

Poll Books

Although Parliament was first summoned in the thirteenth century, and each county or borough returned two members to the Commons, as voted in public by the forty shilling freeholders, the names of voters were not recorded until the end of the seventeenth century. This was because there were fears of corruption. Parliament passed laws to state that books could be published which listed those who had voted in each constituency and the candidates that each had voted for. These books were known as poll books, but they were not published every year. Elections were held at least every three years up to 1715, then every seven years thereafter, but could be held earlier if the government decided. There was an election in 1747, six years after the previous one, because the government estimated it would do better then, which indeed it did. Constituencies were far from equal; with Old Sarum famously having an electorate in single figures whilst Yorkshire had about 15,000 voters, yet each returned two members.

Only a minority of adult men could vote. Yet it has been estimated that, in 1715, about 20 per cent of men aged 21 or more could vote; at the very end of our period, the Reform Act of 1832 increased this number a little. Voting rights depended on a man holding property which yielded a certain annual income.

Poll books then list the men who voted, arranged sometimes by parish, sometimes by alphabetical order of surname, with the candidates they voted for; not always both from the same party. The listings are usually alphabetical within the parish. Some poll books also give the voter's occupation. That for York in 1741 lists these; mostly shopkeepers and craftsmen, but also some working men such as labourers and sedan chair men. You will also learn what your ancestor's political affinity was.

Poll books were only created after a contested election, not every year. And not every election was contested. If opposing politicians could agree to send one member each to Parliament, then there would be no election and thus no poll book.

Poll books are usually to be found in county and borough record offices covering that particular county or city. See Gibson's *Poll Books, 1696–1872*. The best single national collection is held at the Guildhall Library, covering 1696–1868, though with many gaps. The Institute of Historical Research on Malet Street also has a sizeable collection, and is on open access, but entry is restricted unlike at the Guildhall Library.

Pamphlets

Many other published works were created, especially in the eighteenth and nineteenth centuries. There were political tracts and religious sermons, both of which could be very popular indeed. There were also novels by the likes of Samuel Richardson, Henry Fielding and Jane Austen. None of these are of direct genealogical importance, but they indicate what your ancestors may have read, or may have had read to them.

Gentry and Nobility

There are books listing gentry and peerage, which includes their ancestors, in some cases back to the Middle Ages. The first such was *Debrett's Peerage* in 1802, followed by his *Baronetage* of 1808. Subsequent editions were brought out as the century progressed. These two were eventually combined into the one volume. Another series was *Burke's Peerage* of 1826, and published annually from 1847 to 1940, and then irregularly subsequently. *Burke's Landed Gentry* began to be published in 1837, though did not appear as regularly as the *Peerage*. The updated versions of these books included new families who had risen through commerce and other means. However, doubts have been cast on the accuracy of these volumes, with Professor Freeman in 1877 describing the claims made in the latter as 'much wild nonsense'. More recent editions are generally accepted as being more accurate.

These volumes can be found in any good reference library, but larger selections are only available at more specialist libraries and institutions such as TNA. Names are arranged alphabetically. Extinct peerages are excluded, but there have been volumes dedicated to such.

An example from *Burke's Landed Gentry* from 1848 is as follows. The Hereford family of Lambe of Bidney and Henwood was currently headed by William Lambe Esquire. He had been born in 1765, and had married, in 1794, Harriott Mary Welsh of Warwick, whose father was John. She had died in 1804 but had borne her husband six children, all named, with spouses if applicable and whether they had children or not (none named). The second wife of William Lambe was noted, the year of marriage, and her father's name and place of residence. Then the family's lineage is given, which goes back to 1661. Family names, often with years of birth, marriage and death are given. More attention is devoted to names and details of those in direct line of descent.

Famous People

If you think you may have a famous ancestor, try looking in the *Oxford Dictionary of National Biography*, published in 2004, which is all of forty-four volumes (held by good reference libraries), or available online as a subscription site (available free for users at some record offices and libraries). This is the successor to the *Dictionary of National Biography*, produced at the end of the nineteenth century, and the newer version contains far more names. The volumes list tens of thousands of individuals in British history – soldiers, sailors, writers, politicians, scholars, clergymen and criminals to name just a few categories. They are arranged alphabetically and there is an article about each life, of varying length, together with references on which the article is based. The online version is to be preferred for three reasons. First, it is updated in the light of new facts and to correct any errors therein. Secondly, even if you do not have a famous ancestor, you may have someone who was associated with, say, Samuel Pepys, and may be mentioned in the said article, and the online search facility allows you to search by name. You can also search by place, so you could discover if there was anyone famous who lived in the same place as your ancestor or attended the same school or college.

Published sources would seem fairly easy to use, for they are in English, legible and several copies of most exist, making them more accessible than some sources. The major drawback is that they are mostly unindexed, so unless you have a rough idea of the date that a particular event happened, searching blind can be fruitless and lengthy. Secondly, these publications overwhelmingly include the better off in society rather than those with few material goods.

Chapter 8

MANORIAL RECORDS

Manorial records are probably the most single important source for family historians for the centuries prior to the establishment of parish registers in the sixteenth century. They record the largest number of names and include those of people of quite humble social origin, which for this period few other documents, saving the poll tax records, do. However they are probably one of the most underused archives by family historians, partly because some are deterred by the palaeography and Latin, and there is more on this matter in Appendix 1. The manorial records for the place where your immediate post-1538 ancestors resided would be the best place to begin your search.

England was made up of manors in Anglo-Saxon times and this division persisted, albeit with many changes, until its abolition in 1922. William I's famous Domesday survey was a record of manors held in 1086. A manor was a geographical and economic unit of land, and they came in various shapes and sizes. It was not always synonymous with parish. For example, the manor of Fulham, held by the Bishop of London in 1086, was made up of numerous parishes: Acton, Ealing, Chiswick and Fulham. Many of these were subdivided into sub-manors. Manors were not owned, but held by a lord, who might be female or a cleric or a knight. All land was technically held by the monarch, who allocated most of it to the mighty subjects of his realm, bishops and secular lords, in return for their military support. In turn they let out manors to their chief followers, often knights or clergy of the middling rank. Many of these tenants held several manors, and most of these were supervised by a bailiff; few had manor houses which are usually associated with manors.

Each manor was divided into the lord's own land, called the demesne, land that was held by the lord's tenants, and finally common land and wasteland. There were two types of tenant. First, there were the villeins, who worked on the demesne for part of their time, in return for their tenancy. Then there were the freemen who held their tenancies by the payment of a cash rent to the lord. On the tenant's death a sum, known as a heriot, had to be paid to the lord. For the heir to enter into the property, an entry fee, known as a relief, had to be paid to the lord. These tenants often made up the juries in the manorial courts. Some tenants held land by

Frith Manor, Mill Hill, Middlesex. Paul Lang's collection.

both forms of payment. Villein tenure evolved into a copyhold tenancy (so called because both lord and villein had a copy of the latter's title to his tenancy) in which labour services were replaced by rent, a process speeded up by the Black Death of the fourteenth century. Most tenants held land by copyhold tenure, and copyhold land could not be sold. After a tenant's death, the lord could grant it to anyone else or could allow the heir to take

Boscombe Manor. Paul Lang's collection.

76

it over. Much depended on manorial custom, which varied between manors.

Tenants could sub-let part of their land, but this would cease on the death of the sub-tenant, who would often be a cottar or tenant at will, who were lower down in the social hierarchy.

The decline of the manor as a unit, though not as a legal entity, resulted in the parish increasing its powers in the sixteenth century. Some disappeared altogether. One important institution was the manor court, and it was this which produced the crucial records of the manor's tenants and their activities.

Manor Courts

There were two types of manor court. The first was the court baron, or *curia baronis*. It was usually held every three weeks. It concerned the customs of the manor, relating to land tenure and use, and also served to uphold the payment of all dues and services owed to the lord. Disputes between tenants could be settled here, such as complaints of trespass and the settlement of small claims. The court also appointed its own officers, principally the reeve or bailiff who collected the lord's dues, and the hayward, who oversaw the repair of fences and boundaries between landholdings.

Then there was the court leet, or *curia letis*, which was held less often, perhaps twice annually. It dealt with the operation of frankpledge, or *visus franciplegii*. This was a system of mutual responsibility based on a group of about ten households to uphold law and order. The offences it dealt with were common nuisances, affrays and breaking the assize of bread and ale. The latter regulated the sale of goods. The court could fine or imprison offenders. Its principal official was the constable. A fine was called an amercement because the offender was at the court's mercy, and it would decide his penalty. There was a jury of twelve men who possessed property (worth at least £10 per year from 1696).

However, these courts' functions were not always sharply differentiated. They could be held in the lord's hall, or in the open air or in an ecclesiastical building if the lord was a clergyman. Usually the bailiff presided, but occasionally it could be the lord himself. Attendance by villeins was compulsory. Freemen had a greater leeway in attending, but there was no hard and fast rule. This court survived until the sixteenth and seventeenth centuries, though it was superseded by the parish, as noted in Chapter 3.

Manorial documents do not survive before the thirteenth century, though as noted the institution is centuries older. By the end of the century they exist in great quantity, but their survival varies considerably from manor to manor.

These documents are usually set forward in the same way, which makes

Overseer and villeins. Paul Lang's collection.

them easier to deal with once a few have been looked at. For the courts leet, at the top of the parchment roll will be the name of the type of court, the day of the week and the date. Then there will be the list of penalties paid by those tenants who did not attend the court. Those non-attendees who did not send apologies were given heavier fines (known as amercements). Then there is a list of changes in tenancy, including surrenders and admissions, and details of entry fines paid. When a tenant died, this would be noted and his heir named in what is known as an inquisition post mortem (about property, not on how the individual died). They would have their right acknowledged and would pay a forfeit, often in the shape of a beast, termed a heriot. There may also be a list of witnesses. There should also be a little information about the individual who inherited the land, with his age, and proofs given by witnesses of this fact. Other new tenants, who purchased their tenancy, would also be named here. Descriptions of property were often given.

For the years just after 1348, the impact of the Black Death may be noted, but the records are not explicit. For example, they may state that land has been passed to someone from another who has died.

For courts baron, there is a list of disputes to be dealt with, with names, detail of offence and penalty paid by the offenders. There may also be a list of the court jury and officials present. Court rolls for Ruislip Manor, for example, show that in 1246, Isabella, Peter's widow, was fined 18d for her son John's trespassing in the lord's wood. Hugh Tree's beasts were in the lord's garden and he was fined 6d, whilst Walter Hill and Hugh Slipper stood as his securities. In a later court roll, it was stated that Lucy Mill had committed adultery and had her property seized by the manor.

A court roll for the manor of Northolt for 1508 reads as follows, and shows the information that can be obtained therein.

Headboroughs say that John Hacche, and Edward Romyn owe suit of Court and are in default, each fined 2d.

John Rous is a brewer of ale and break the assize. 4d.

John Gybbes has allowed his beasts to trespass in the corn fields of the tenants of the manor, fined 3d.

A ram has been found straying, a proclamation to be made.

Alice Tonnell, widow who holds copyhold land of two half virgates, one called 'Shepards' and the other 'Hillers' lying diversely in the common fields of Northall has surrendered them to the use of John Gybbes who does not attend, ordered to attend the next court under penalty.

Humfry Hegger, brother of John Hegger, son of William Hegger aged 11 years wishes to be admitted to a messuage and a virgate of land which was held by John Hegger when he died. Humfry is admitted but the land is to be held by George Hegger until Humfry is aged 24 years. Fine 20d.

George Stevyns who holds of the lord a tenement and 3 acres of land, one acre in 'Tymlowe feld', one acre in 'Estfeld' abutting on 'Longe Furlong' and three acres lying next to 'Shirwyns croft' has surrendered to the use of John Rous. Fine paid.

Margery the wife of John Cokke has a ditch containing 30 perches, fine 6d.

Apart from these court records, known as court rolls, there were less common documents.

Rentals and Extents

These are far less common than court rolls. Rentals and surveys of the manor which were only made from time to time, often when the manor changed hands, and these documents, as with the court rolls, often list people, describe the nature of their tenure, the services they rendered to the lords and describe their holdings. For urban parishes, street names are often given. Property descriptions are sometimes given.

Minute books and draft court rolls can be useful substitutes when the original court rolls do not exist. Suit books and call books list those who attended.

Other manorial records include accounts, but these rarely mention individuals, rather the sums of money accruing from various agricultural products. Custumals might be more useful, for they list the rents, services and obligations owed by tenants to the lord. However few were created

Villeins fattening pigs. Paul Lang's collection.

after the mid-fourteenth century; and in many manors, oral testimony was relied on instead of the written record.

In order to track down the whereabouts of such documents, use the Manorial Documents Register, which is currently incomplete, but work is ongoing to complete the national coverage. Yorkshire, Middlesex, Hampshire, Surrey and Norfolk are included amongst others. It can be searched online at www.nationalarchives.gov.uk/mdr. The London Metropolitan Archive holds the archives of many manors in Middlesex, but some are held at TNA, especially manors held by the Crown and elsewhere; the colleges of the two ancient universities held several manors in southern England and so the library of a particular college may be a place you might have to visit. Westminster Abbey muniments room holds some. Some are in private hands.

Some manorial court rolls have been transcribed and so are more easily accessible for most researchers – some for early fifteenth-century Harrow are found with the originals at the LMA for instance. Some record societies have also transcribed some medieval court rolls. For those which are not translated, a useful guide is Denis Stuart's *Manorial Records* (1992). It contains a number of exercises for the student to practise upon, as well as a handy dictionary of terms often found therein.

However, it is worth remembering that manorial tenure continued up to 1922, so there are manorial records which are written in English and so are easier to use. Not all survive, but for some manors there are centuries worth of records in existence.

Not every inhabitant of manors is listed in these records. Women and children are less likely to appear. Nor are servants or the poorest likely to be listed. However about three-quarters of adult male tenants do.

Tenants of Crown lands can be identified in the Parliamentary Survey of Crown Lands of 1649 and 1650, in TNA, E317, which describes land held by the said tenants. Sales of land are in CRES39/67–74 and E320.

Inquisitions post mortem occurred prior to 1660. When a landholder died, there had to be an enquiry held by the royal escheator (the King's local representative) of the county. This would determine what land was held under what terms, would note the former landholder and decide who the successor was. Records are at TNA, C132–42 and at E149–50, which cover 1236–1660.

Manorial archives prior to the sixteenth century are the best single type of records for family historians as they record the largest numbers of names, though as noted they are far from comprehensive. They do, however, present the best chance of finding ancestors prior to parish registers. Having located ancestors in the earliest parish registers you can, these should be your next port of call. Hopefully there will be court rolls for the manors in the parish where your ancestors dwelt.

Chapter 9

PROPERTY RECORDS

Property is and was a key source of wealth and thus power. Recording its ownership and changes in its status and owners has been of prime importance throughout the centuries. Indeed, in the twelfth century, forged deeds for ecclesiastical property became commonplace. The survival of deeds is another matter. From the whole of the centuries of Saxon England, only 2,000 survive; but in the thirteenth century alone there are tens of thousands. It has been estimated that the latter estimate is but the tip of the iceberg of perhaps eight million which were created. In the Saxon era, most deeds issued from the monarch, whereas in the twelfth century private deeds were created, but this explosion of documentation resulted from even peasants being accustomed to the use of documents in property transactions. More and more, society was relying on the written word rather than the oral tradition, and this is good news for historians.

Houses opposite church, Saffron Walden, 2011. Author's collection.

Another boon is that in 1199 the clerks of the Chancery, a key department of the King's government, began keeping copies of all the charters they issued. Most of what we know about property is when it changed hands and so there was a need to record what had happened.

There is no one set of records for this period to property on a national scale. After 1837 there are several: tithe apportionments, Land Valuations and the Farm Survey for instance. Instead there is a variety of source material for the propertied Englishman. Remember that many adults – servants and labourers, for instance – did not own property, and that female owners were a distinct minority.

Deeds

Since the Middle Ages, deeds have been drawn up to legally convey property (technically hereditaments) from one party to another. A deed involves at least two parties. Initially two copies of the document were created on the same piece of parchment and then they were cut along a wavy line, so if there were any doubts as to the authenticity of the deed, the two could be matched up. There are three types of land: freehold, which is owned for an indefinite period, leasehold, which is for a limited duration, and copyhold, which is held from a manor by special tenure.

With the increase of the middle class deeds reached their peak in the nineteenth century, with many being created and kept. Until 1925 it was necessary to retain all deeds relating to a property, and these ever growing bundles were passed on to each new purchaser. However, owing to changes in the law of property in the twentieth century, it is no longer necessary to retain deeds going back more than fifteen years before the present owner acquires the property. Banks and solicitors have no need to retain vast numbers of deeds. This has resulted in a great many collections of deeds finding their way into local authority record offices, often via the agency of the British Records Association, which acts as a clearing house for the distribution of archives. Many other deeds were simply thrown away; some ended up as lampshade covers and others can sometimes be found in secondhand bookshops.

These deeds can cover decades of a house's history from the moment the builder or developer buys the plot of land, through changes of ownership, and increasing prices. A deed can be a very lengthy document, if it was drawn up from the mid-eighteenth century to the mid-nineteenth (usually these are made from parchment), before being reduced to a more manageable size as the nineteenth century progressed. Abstracts of Title are not deeds but are a summary of deeds relating to that particular piece of land from earliest times to date, so are extremely useful if the original deeds do not survive.

Post-medieval deeds begin with the names, addresses and occupations

Blagrove House, Barnard Castle. Paul Lang's collection.

of those selling the property (this may be several names, such as a man and his wife), then the same information for the buyers (or tenants). There then may be a recital of previous deeds, listing previous owners, before stating the current price/rent, and then listing what the property consists of, such as the grounds and any outbuildings. Any restrictions on the property will be noted – for instance, not using the property as commercial premises. Finally there will usually be the signatures of witnesses to the deed. Expect deeds to be parchment and if dated before 1733 they will usually be written in Latin. Dating is by regnal year, i.e. the year after the current monarch's accession. So a deed from February 1728 will be one dated in the first year of the reign of George II. Charles II counted his regnal year from the death of his father in 1649, not when he actually became king in 1660, so there are no deeds for the first eleven years of his reign. That said, most deeds prior to about 1300 are not dated, so the only clue comes from the people mentioned in the deed. For nineteenth-century deeds, the date is given in the form recognizable to modern readers and the text is in English. Medieval deeds are generally far more concise.

Many deed collections are, as stated, held at local authority record offices. They are usually well catalogued, which is a skill archivists are taught in some detail on their training courses. But the number of deeds originally created was so vast that the thousands of deeds in record offices represent only a fraction of these, and a researcher may not be fortunate enough to locate what they are looking for. As with any archives, a search by person/property on the access to archives (a2a) database is worth trying (it can be found on TNA's website).

Several counties possess deeds registries, in which property transactions were registered. These are for Middlesex (1709–1938) and the ridings of Yorkshire (1704–1972 for the West Riding, 1736–1972 for the North Riding and 1708–1976 for the East Riding). These are huge collections, not of deeds, but of a summary of each one (there are some complete transcripts for some of the later ones). They are indexed by year by the name of the seller, not the address of the property. With the year of sale and the seller, you can then check the indexes to the deeds registry (on microfilm) to uncover the reference numbers for the actual summary of the deed. For the West Riding, there are 1.5 million deed summaries from 1704–1915. However, registration of deeds was not compulsory. Leases of less than twenty-one years were not recorded. Copyhold transactions were also omitted.

There are many types of deed, and we shall now examine them one by one.

A common form of deed in the feet of fine, which dates from the twelfth century to 1833. This was a tripartite agreement, with both seller and buyer having copies. The third copy went to the Court of Common Pleas and surviving copies are located at TNA. They are indexed at IND1/7233–44 and 1/7217–68. Many have been published by county record societies (available at county record offices and TNA).

Common recoveries were developed in the fifteenth century. They converted property from fee tail (where it cannot be sold) to fee simple (which can be sold). The buyer brought an action against the landholder, claiming the land was his and that he wished to 'recover' it. This was a legal fiction. The first party appointed a third party to represent them in court. However he would then default and so judgment went to the second party enabling them to acquire the property as fee simple. The first party would in reality sell the land to the second party. Up to 1583, judgments were entered into the plea rolls at TNA, CP40, indexed in CP60. From 1583 these

are found in CP43, with indexes at IND1/17183–216. For the palatine jurisdictions, see CHES29 (Plea Rolls, 1259–1830), CHES31 (recoveries,
1280–1830), CHES32 (recoveries enrolments, 1585–1703), DURH13
(1344–1845) and PL15 (1401–1848).

Leases were common from the seventeenth century onwards. They were
a method of converting copyhold land to leasehold. A lease often lasted for
the lives of three named persons (thus providing useful family names), and
was obtained by the payment of an entry sum and then an annual rent.
Further lives could be entered on the payment of another entry sum.
Sometimes leases were for just a few years, sometimes for hundreds of
years. There is also the lease and release; in the former the purchaser pays
a nominal sum only for a lease of but a year, and then takes a release in
which the real money changes hands. These documents are usually found
together and cease to exist in 1845.

Another major form of deed, from 1536, was the bargain and sale. The
first party bargained and sold the property to the second. The first party
retained legal possession, but the use of the land was with the second party,
in exchange for payment. The latter also had to pay rent to the lord of the
manor, too. All these forms of transaction had to be enrolled with the Clerk

Gift of John de Chaisneto, c.1147. Author's collection.

of Quarter Sessions, and so these enrolments, though not the deeds themselves, should be found at the appropriate county record office.

Patent rolls record grants of land from the Crown, and are found at TNA, C66, for the period 1485–1946. There are manuscript indexes in C274. Many patent rolls have been calendared, especially from the fourteenth to the seventeenth century.

Marriage settlements also concern property, though were usually restricted to the upper echelons of society. They are frighteningly large and bulky documents. Their essential purpose is to convey property to the newly married couple in a way that did not lead to the husband acquiring the whole of the bride's portion, as legally all a married woman's property belonged to her husband. Therefore the capital was given to a third party made up of trustees, so that the husband could only touch the interest or rents. As a lecturer in archives once noted, 'Lawyers were an absolutely essential part of any eighteenth-century romance.'

You don't always need to read every line of a deed, because repetition and legal phraseology often take up much of it. Instead you can scan the deed for names, places and sums of money. Much of this essential information may already be in the catalogue description, thus saving the researcher much work. This is especially the case if the deed is difficult to decipher.

Surveys

The Domesday Book of 1086 is a record of landholding, and is the most famous work produced by the Norman administration. It notes who held which manors and often who was the previous landholder (often a deceased Saxon nobleman). There are many published transcripts of it, some of which are indexed, and copies should be available at most large libraries and on TNA website. Yet not all of the country was included: the City of London and most of the north of England were not However Middlesex was, as were other counties adjoining London, now parts of Greater London. Only the major tenants are included, so the number of names is minimal. Yet if you suspect that your ancestor might have been a major landowner in the late eleventh century, it is worth a look.

The following is for the manor of West Twyford, Middlesex:

> In Twyford, Durand, a canon of St. Paul, holds of the King two hides of land. There is land to one plough and a half. There are three villeins there of half a hide, and half a virgate. Pasture for the cattle of the village. Pannage for one hundred pigs. This land is worth thirty shillings; the same when received; in the time of King Edward, twenty shillings.
>
> In the same village, Gueri, a canon of St. Paul's, holds two hides of

land. There is land to one plough and a half. There is a plough in the demesne, and a half may be made. There are two villeins of one virgate and one border of six acres; and three cottagers. Pannage for fifty pigs. The land is worth thirty shillings; the same when received, in the time of King Edward twenty shillings. This land belonged and does belong to the Church of St. Paul, in the demesne of the canons.

A Domesday survey was made of parts of the north of England in the following century, called the Boldern Survey.

There were less-known surveys of landholders, too. The Ladies Roll or Rotuli de Dominabus of 1185 was one, and this included the county of Middlesex. It listed lands held by female landholders, mostly widows and daughters of tenants in chief (i.e. those who held land directly from the monarch). Minors were also included. A printed transcript was published by the Pipe Roll Society in 1913. In the following century, a Book of Fees, which was a collection of records from 1198–1293, relating to land tenure throughout England, was created. It is arranged year by year and then by county. You can see the original at TNA (E164/5–6), but it is easier to use the transcription found in *The Book of Fees*, a three-volume series published by HMSO between 1920 and 1931.

There are other medieval surveys, such as those for Worcestershire, Winchester, Lincolnshire, Northamptonshire and Leicestershire for the early twelfth century. All have been published and list landowners and their landholdings. The book *Doomsday Descendants* lists people from these documents and others from 1066–1166. The Boldon Book of 1183 includes the tenants of the Bishop of Durham and there is a translation in the VCH for Durham, vol. 1.

Moving forward in time, there are the Hundred Rolls, from 1255–80. These listed individual landholders in each manor, but also included the names of jurors and bailiffs, as well as their land and how much they were paying for it. Sometimes even unfree tenants were listed. As Edward I himself noted, it was meant to be 'fuller and more detailed than the survey carried out by the Conqueror'. Although not all the returns have survived for all the counties, the surviving returns are to be found in the second of the two-volume *Rotuli Hundredorum* (1818). This is in Latin, but has an index to names and places.

Valuations

These were often drawn up by the parish in order to assess the value of property for rating purposes. They list landowners/occupiers, the extent of their land, what it was used for (arable or meadowland) and its value. For some larger properties, lists of fields (named) and buildings may be given. The 1821 valuation of Norwood notes that John Venables was owner and occupier of a dwelling house-cum-grocer's shop in Southall, valued at £8. Eldred Dodson owned property on Frog Green, 'a dwelling house, barn, a stable, shed, yard, garden and orchard'. There was meadowland to the extent of one acre, two rods and thirty perches, and the entire value was put at £15. If you're lucky there may be a map which has numbers linking it to the valuation list.

Enclosure Records

From the sixteenth to the nineteenth century there was an agricultural revolution in the English countryside. The medieval system of strip fields was replaced by one in which land was parcelled out into discrete lots. This was done by enclosing land. Commons and waste land were also enclosed. In the eighteenth century the most common method to effect this change was by Parliamentary Act. This resulted in documentation being drawn up to show who owned and who occupied what part of the land of any one parish.

These were chiefly the Enclosure Award and a map, often the first ever drawn up of many parishes. The award lists those people who were allotted land and how much land they received. The maps show where these lands actually were. Most of these maps and awards are now held with the appropriate county record office or borough archives. For some of the later Enclosure Acts of 1801 and 1836, the awards are now held at TNA in record series C54 and E13. Awards do not list all parishioners, nor all householders therein, merely those, usually the better off, who were recipients of land. Day labourers, for instance, would be excluded. In some cases, only part of the land in the parish was enclosed and in some parishes none was, such as urban parishes.

Forfeited Estates Commission

Following the failure of the Jacobite rebellion of 1715, estates of the defeated Jacobite nobility and gentry were forfeit to the Crown, and a high proportion of these families were Catholic. These estates were chiefly in Northumberland and Lancashire, which were the two major sources of the minimal English Jacobite support that roused itself into action, though these men also owned land in adjacent counties such as Yorkshire and Cumberland. Surveys of landownership and tenancy details were made by the commissioners. Thus an examination of these unindexed papers, all held at TNA, in FEC1 and 2, can reveal details about lands held, owners, tenants, land values and rentals, with records sometimes going back to the sixteenth century.

Royalist Composition Papers

The unfortunate royalists of the 1640s and 1650s were not only losers in the political and military struggles of those decades, but were hit financially, too. In 1643 the Parliamentary Committee for the Sequestration of Delinquents' Estates was formed to take their lands (no wonder that royalist John Evelyn spent much of the 1640s abroad). Even when the war was over, the victors showed limited clemency. In 1653, the Committee for Compounding the Estates of Royalists and Delinquents was formed. Those royalists who pledged their loyalty to the new order were allowed to pay fines to maintain their lands, on a scale depending on their involvement in the past war. Records of the said committees are at TNA, series SP20 and 23. Yorkshire Composition papers were published in the *Yorkshire Archaeological Record Series* for 1893 and 1895.

Estate Papers

The large estates held by the church, nobility and gentry often give details of the properties that these estates were subdivided into. Information about tenants and the lands rented from the owner are often copious. Rentals and land surveys were occasionally undertaken in order to assess the estate's value and extent. There may also be plans of the estate properties. These archives survive in county record offices; some may still be held by the estate if it is still in existence, and so access might be difficult.

Gift of Walter de Clive of property in London, 1289. Author's collection.

Inquisitions post mortem were held on the death of one of the monarch's major tenants by the King's escheator or his deputy. They had to establish the extent of the estate and the rightful heir. A jury assisted in the process. Records are held at TNA in C133–42 and in E149–50, and survive in most numbers from 1270–1350. Various calendars and indexes exist; some county record series have published those for their county. The National Registry of Archives lists what exists and can be accessed on TNA's website.

Auctions and Sales Catalogues

For substantial houses and estates, published lists detailing property, perhaps with a plan, were created, especially from the eighteenth century onwards, if these were to be sold, often on the owner's death. These can be very precise, stating the contents of each room, even down to listing the books and wines, as well as works of art and more mundane furniture. They will usually be found in county and borough record offices, often along solicitors' papers, and should be catalogued by the deceased's name as well as the property's name. They will tell a lot about the owner's tastes and wealth, though they will not note who bought what. There is also a collection of auction catalogues at TNA, in J46, and these can be searched for on the catalogue.

Sales or rentals of property are often advertised in local newspapers and it has been suggested that, in the eighteenth century, this was their prime local function. Apart from giving the price, they will usually give a brief description of the property.

Insurance

From the seventeenth century it became possible to insure one's property from damage; primarily fire. The Great Fire of London destroyed much of the City in 1666 and this prompted the existence of such companies and helped supply a demand for them. Initially insurance companies were based in London but very soon they had agents elsewhere in England. These included the Sun, Royal Exchange and Phoenix. They often established their own fire brigades and their clients' properties were identified by special markings.

Policy registers are the chief form of documentation which was created. They will list client, address, occupation, location of insured property, its contents, value and type of construction. Information about tenants if any would also be provided. Policy dates and premiums paid will also be noted. The records will be arranged in chronological order. There may or may not be indexes (contemporary or more recent). County record offices should hold papers of provincial insurance companies. Records for those of the Royal Exchange and Hand in Hand are held at the London Metropolitan Archives, and the two former cover the whole country. Another major firm was the Sun and its records are at the Guildhall Library. The Phoenix, which also had a national coverage, has deposited its records at Cambridge University Library. Westminster Fire Office's records are at Westminster Archives.

Maps

Cities and major towns have been mapped from the early seventeenth century. However, from the eighteenth and nineteenth centuries there are also many maps of small towns and villages. There are enclosure maps, of course, but there were many others, too. These feature most if not all of the properties in a parish. They might name houses and streets, prominent buildings such as public houses, schools and churches, as well as the houses of any nobility and the resident gentry. Even if your ancestor is not mentioned therein, these maps will give an insight into the immediate world in which they would have moved. From 1801 there are Ordnance Survey maps at one inch to the mile, but their coverage was only national by the 1860s. There may be maps of places showing particular events; the earliest one of Preston dates from 1715 depicting the battle there. Maps showing roads and the settlements they intersected were drawn by the turnpike companies in the eighteenth century. Maps can be found at county and borough record offices and libraries; there are also significant collections at the British Library and TNA. Some have been published and copies can be bought; sometimes they appear in published local histories.

Other Records

Don't forget that poll books (see Chapter 7), hearth tax records and rate books (see Chapter 10) are also useful sources for the history of property. However, these rarely mention the exact address, as they are primarily concerned with listing individuals, whether voters or taxpayers. Wills and administrations are another good source for identifying property, but this was only what was held in later life, and were often vague.

Property records can tell a lot about an individual or family. First, they can indicate what they owned or held at a certain point in time, whether they were buyer, seller or tenant. This is often indicative of wealth. But they can also provide information about family relationships and others known to them. They can help pin down where someone lived at a precise moment in time.

Chapter 10

TAXATION

Benjamin Franklin once famously observed that there is nothing certain in life except for 'death and taxes'. This is just as well for family historians, and this chapter will concentrate on taxes, the less well-known genealogical source. Governments at both local and national level always need sources of revenue in order to pay for their policies and, in the process of their administration, records of taxpayers are made and often retained to be used by researchers. Yet in the Middle Ages only a small proportion of royal revenue came from taxation (15% in the twelfth century, for instance). This chapter looks at financial levies imposed by national and local government since the seventeenth century. It was in this century that taxation became permanent; hitherto, the monarchs only asked money from their subjects when they needed to go to war. How accurate the records are is another question, for it was in the taxpayers' interests to try to reduce their liability by evasion or avoidance. There are a number of different types of tax; those on property, those on wealth, those on income and those on expenditure. The last type (indirect taxes, such as customs and excise) can be disregarded because they are not taxes on individuals, but on spending and therefore lead to no records of individuals. Most of the tax records will list the taxpayer and the amount they paid or/and were assessed at, and most are organized by county then manor/parish, and there should be a date of assessment.

Readers should recall that in the currency of England from Saxon times until decimalization of 1971 twelve pence equalled one shilling and that twenty shillings made one pound.

Poll Tax

Although there were no regularly imposed taxes or rates in the Middle Ages, monarchs did need their subjects' money from time to time, especially to fight wars against the French and Scots. Occasional taxes, or subsidies or levies, were imposed from the thirteenth century onwards. The most well-known were the poll taxes of the early years of the reign of Richard II (1377–81) which helped lead to the Peasants' Revolt of 1381. These were taxes, usually set at a flat rate, on all adult men, with a few

List of Brading ratepayers in Isle of Wight 1765. Author's collection.

exceptions, such as servants. Women did not pay. There was no variation for income or wealth. Apart from creating outrage amongst many, they also resulted in lists of most of England's male population being created, organized by county. Relationships in families and occupations are sometimes given. What is even better is that these lists have been transcribed and published in three volumes (by Dr Carolyn Fenwick) so should be available at the British Library and Guildhall Library, inter alia. The originals are at TNA, while some county record offices, such as Essex, have microfilm copies. We should note that returns do not exist for every village, but when they do, they list men, their wives and children aged above 14.

It is often forgotten that the poll tax made a reappearance in the seventeenth century. Seven were raised in all: in 1660, 1667, 1678, 1689, 1691, 1694 and 1697. Records survive for the last four assessments. As ever, it was a tax on people, including both householders and lodgers, and sometimes children, but exempting paupers. The records are to be found at TNA, in class E182, arranged by county, then by hundred, then by parish. The amount levied depended on the social status and occupation. The LMA has a transcribed copy of the assessment for the City for 1692.

Subsidies

There were other taxes levied in the Middle Ages, of course, and some of these records survive. They were known as 'Lay Subsidies'; these were not paid by the church (though clergymen owning land in their own right were liable). These were usually levied because the monarch needed money in wartime and were paid at a fraction of the individual's moveable goods. They were levied for a particular stated purpose. Those which survive exist at TNA and date from 1275–1525, though not every year by any means; there were none in the fifteenth century, for example. For many of these levies, only total sums owed by place are noted. Yet there are names given for some of the levies in the late thirteenth and early fourteenth centuries, and also in 1524, when land was taxed at 20% and moveable goods at 28% and, because payment thresholds were low, most adult men were assessed and so named in these records. Because there was widespread evasion,

b. Henry VIII. York Groat bearing Wolsey's initials and Cardinal's Hat.

a. Henry VIII. Tournay Groat, 1513.

c. Henry VIII. Gold George noble, c. 1526.

The fruits of taxation: coins from the time of Henry VIII.
Paul Lang's collection.

very full lists were compiled for both 1523 and 1543, both of which are at TNA. Tax records can be found at TNA in E179, but also at county record offices. For example, Essex Record Office holds transcripts of three lay subsidy returns for the fourteenth century and one for 1524–5. Two of these have been indexed and one has been translated. Some have been published, including those for Devonshire for 1323 and for Gloucestershire for 1327.

Foreign merchants were taxed on numerous occasions in the fifteenth and early sixteenth centuries; the sums levied were known as Alien Subsidies. TNA, E179 contains lists of taxpayers, especially for 1440 and 1483–4, but there were numerous exemptions and evasions; the Irish were not liable after 1442, for instance. Taxes levied were a tax on alien house-holders (16d p.a.) and on non-householders (6d p.a.). Returns for Southwark have been calendared by J L Bolton, *The Alien Communities of London in the Fifteenth Century* (1998), and the same historian has also calen-dared the Alien Subsidy Roll for London for 1483 (E179/242/25) and for Middlesex for 1484 (E179/141/94–5). TNA also holds records of taxation paid by the medieval Jewish community prior to their expulsion in 1290, but no one has been able to trace a line of descent from these people.

Rates

The longest running of all levies in England, lasting from 1601 to 1990, were the rates. These were first imposed periodically in the later sixteenth century, but as a result of the Elizabethan (Old) Poor Law Act of 1601 usually became a regular annual fixture, though not always – the parish of Lee in Kent had so few poor that an annual rate was unnecessary. There could also be additional temporary rates levied on parishes, for example to finance a county prison or asylum. Normally, though, rates were levied in order that the parish could relieve the local poor in cash or in goods. The vestry would set the annual rate at a certain level at so many shillings in the pound and the overseers of the parish would assess the value of each property in the parish. These assessments would then be listed in the rate book, with the figure payable next to the ratepayer's name. Each rate book usually covers several years' assessments, depending on the size of the parish's population, at least until the early nineteenth century. We are thus presented with a list of householders for each year, in a series of books, potentially from the early seventeenth century to the early nineteenth century. Furthermore, it is possible to see how valuable that ancestor's property was compared to others in the parish. There were also separate rates levied for the upkeep of the church fabric, known as the church rate, and the highway rate, to pay for men to repair roads and bridges in the parish. Every property was assessed, except of those who were too poor to pay and who were in receipt of poor relief (their names are usually featured in books of overseers' disbursement, as noted in Chapter 4). There is usually a note to state whether the rates were paid.

Defaulters are also listed in a separate section at the end of a particular year or half year's rates, with the amount that was still outstanding.

However, there are two caveats. The first is that the survival of a large run of rate books is very rare. For example, those for Hampstead parish only cover the years 1774, 1777, 1779–1826, 1829–55, but those for Holborn exist from 1729–1900, with very few gaps. One example of a run beginning in the seventeenth century is those for Ealing, 1673–1834, and even then, the first rate book is titled 'volume 37' – the preceding thirty-six having not survived. The sheer bulk and number of rate books for each year for the later nineteenth and twentieth centuries have led many rate books to be destroyed (because of storage restrictions) and so often only rate books for every other year, or every third or fourth year have survived. During the Second World War, the beaming mayor of Croydon gave an early Victorian rate book to the salvage drive to be pulped for the war effort!

Secondly, the rate books usually do not give any clue to the precise whereabouts of the property or give addresses or name the property, in the parish. That said, some rate books, from the eighteenth century, do sometimes break the parish down into different sections. That for Ealing groups ratepayers as to whether they lived around Haven Green, Little Ealing, Castlebar, Gunnersbury, Ealing Common, Church Ealing and so forth, and using the 1777 parish map we can see where these places were. In the assessments for 1753 and 1754 we see the author Henry Fielding's name and in those for 1808–12 there is the Right Honourable Spencer Perceval, Prime Minister. Those for Deptford after 1730 give full addresses, as do those in the City and Westminster.

The Norwood rate book beginning the year of 1653 uses the following preamble, 'An Assessment made the 23rd day of May 1653 for the relief of the aged and impotent poor people of the parish of Norwood for the whole year aforesaid'. There then is a list of names and sums assessed. Most of those listed are men, but there are a few widows, such as 'Elizabeth Child, wid., 0-7-3.' Ranks of some male ratepayers are given, such as 'Robert Awsiter, gent, 1-0-0'. Occasionally the addition 'and sonnes' might appear, too.

Rate books, where they survive, tend to be found in local authority record offices with the parish archives, and at the county record offices. Few have been transcribed, indexed or digitalized. However it is important to note that these rate books were maintained each year, so enable researchers to pinpoint householders during years in which they otherwise could not be traced.

Hearth Tax

Another useful source for the later seventeenth century are the records of the hearth tax. This was a tax imposed on householders from 1662 until 1689. It was payable twice a year in two instalments. Taxpayers had to pay one shilling per hearth, i.e. fireplace, in their property. As with the rates, owners with larger properties had to pay more and the poorest were exempt, as were buildings which were for charitable uses. Constables and overseers had to collect the tax, and there is a high survival rate of hearth tax returns for 1662–6 and for 1669–72. The assessments for the other years do not exist because the tax collection was farmed out to private individuals who did not have to send their returns to the Exchequer.

These assessments are to be found at the TNA in class E179, though some are held locally as parish officials retained a copy for their own use. They are arranged by parish, then present a list of taxpayers and the number of hearths that they are liable to pay for. As with the rates, there is no indica-

A source of seventeenth-century taxation: hearth at the Old House, Hertford. Paul Lang's collection.

tion where in the parish the property is, nor are the poorest householders listed as they were not liable to pay. That said, Essex Record Office have a list of returns for 1671 which include the names of those who were too poor to be chargeable. But they do give an accurate list of most of the householders in the parish and their approximate relative wealth. We can learn that Dr Brabourne had, in 1664–72 a house with nine hearths in Northolt, whereas a neighbour, John Winch had a house with only one chimney.

The number of names in these assessments varies enormously with the number of households in the parish. Greenwich parish assessments (available at Greenwich Local History Library) for 1662–4 include about 6,000 names, whereas those for Isleworth from 1664–74 number 960 and can be found at the Society of Genealogists' Library.

Some hearth tax assessments have been transcribed and so are easily available; but only for a few parishes. If your ancestors lived in Surrey, these have been transcribed and published; likewise those for a number of Middlesex parishes, including Acton, Ealing, Harrow, Hanwell, Perivale, Staines and Northolt, as well as for a number of City parishes and the Kent parishes for 1662 have also been transcribed and indexed.

Information given is the name of the property owner and the number of hearths, which indicates the size of the house. If it was empty, the owner's name is still given, and the fact that the house is empty is noted.

A useful list of what survives, and its whereabouts, can be found in J S Gibson, *The Hearth Tax and Other Later Stuart Tax Lists.*

Tithes

Since the Middle Ages, landowners and householders were obliged to pay tithes to the rector or vicar. These were goods; when the Revd Gold found himself in difficulties with his parishioners in Hayes in the early 1530s, it was over their presenting him with a tenth of the harvest crop. In 1836 the Tithe Commutation Act decreed that this payment should be in cash, and so each parish was assessed. Lists, known as apportionments, detailing landowners and tenants, with acreage, usage (arable, pasture, etc.) and value, were listed. What was even more valuable is that maps of each parish were made and so it is possible to locate where land was owned/rented. Three copies were made; one copy can be found at TNA (IR29 is the series for apportionments, IR30 for the maps), one at the LMA (in its role as diocesan record office) and one may be found at the local authority record office and sometimes parish churches retain them.

The Ship Tax

This was a form of taxation levied on several occasions during 1634–40 and is sometimes cited as a tax which was so unpopular that it led to the outbreak of hostilities between King and Parliament in 1642. It was raised to pay for naval defence. Records are held at TNA, SP16 and 17. Essex Record Office has a transcript for the 1637 return, which has been indexed and lists 15,000 names. However, few assessments survive (there are none for Middlesex) and those which do are organized by county.

The Free and Voluntary Present

This was not 'what it says on the tin', but actually a list of about 130,000 people, with occupations, who gave money to the restored King Charles II in 1661. It is to be found in TNA, E179.

Window Tax

This was assessed from 1696 to 1851 on properties with six or more windows, being charged at two shillings per window. Collectors' assessment books exist for Finsbury and part of Clerkenwell for 1797–8 and 1807–8 at the LMA (TC). These list inhabitants and sums due. There are window tax assessments for Dagenham at Essex Record Office for 1785. Their existence is very partial indeed.

Game Duty

In 1784 and 1785, each person qualified to kill, hunt and sell game, such as gentlemen and gamekeepers, had to register with the clerk of the peace, who would issue a certificate in return for a fee. The clerk had then to transmit an annual account of certificates issued to the Commissioners of Stamp Duty. There are registers at the LMA for those in Middlesex for 1784–1808 and Westminster 1799–1803. There is an alphabetical list for 1784–1807. Essex Record Office has registers for 1784–1806.

The Land Tax

With the abolition of the hearth tax, the government, needing money to fight the war against France, imposed another tax. This commenced from 1692 and was maintained until 1963. As the name suggests, it was a tax on land and so, as with the rates, difficult to evade or avoid. It was levied at a certain number of shillings per £1 of the land's value. In wartime, it could rise to four shillings, but in peacetime was usually one or two shillings (often for political reasons). Surviving assessment lists for Middlesex, covering 1767 and 1780–1832 and for Westminster for 1767, 1781, 1797–1832 are at the LMA. For the City of London, their survival is even better – there are 522 volumes covering 1692–4 and 1703–1949, also at the LMA. Essex Record Office has assessments from 1780–1832, and those for

1782 have been indexed (there are 20,000 names). They also have lists of land tax payers for the Havering Hundred in 1692. Kent lists survive at the county record office from the 1720s. Some, however, exist at local authority record offices, with assessments for Hackney existing for 1727–1824 (with gaps). There are also some for Edmonton (1750) at Enfield Archives and for St George in the East (1801) at Tower Hamlets Archives. The reason why some land tax records do not survive is because, until 1780, land tax records did not have to be returned to the clerk of the peace; afterwards they had to because they were needed for electoral purposes.

From 1798, landowners could pay a lump sum to indemnify themselves against later payments of this tax. The records can be found at TNA in the series IR23, which is arranged by county, then parish, then individual. It lists the landowners' tenants and contract number. Using this number, series IR24 can then be checked, which will give the acreage and where the owners lived. Land tax records are organized by parish, then, for an urban district, by street (but no street number is given).

We should also remember the Land Tax Redemption Office's Quotas and Assessments (TNA, IR23), which lists all property owners in England and Wales in 1798–9. Property owners are listed by parish.

Miscellaneous Taxes and Duties

There were a number of short-lived taxes. One was the marriage duty tax, imposed from 1695–1706 on bachelors aged over 25 and childless widowers. There are lists of City taxpayers for 1695 (only) at the LMA.

Carriage duty was a tax imposed from 1747–82, and lists of payers and

Harlech Castle: medieval taxes often paid for defence expenditure.
Paul Lang's collection.

defaulters can be found at TNA for 1753–66 at T47/2–4. Clearly those listed were those who were fairly wealthy, but if you believe your ancestor was among this happy number, it is worth taking a look at these sources. Likewise, lists of those paying servant tax in 1780 (the tax was introduced in 1777 and in force until 1852) can be found, arranged by county, then parish at TNA in class T47/8. Those not paying, or paying in arrears for 1777–1830, are listed in E182. There are also householders' returns for this tax for Clerkenwell residents for 1798–9 located at the LMA. Another tax for the late eighteenth century which was aimed at the better off in society was on hair powder. Hairpowder duty registers for 1795–7 exist at Essex Record Office, giving names of payers of duty, arranged by parish, listing their occupations and status.

There were also a number of periodic subsidies levied by governments in the sixteenth and seventeenth centuries and records of some of those assessed for these survive. Many of these can be found in the TNA in class E179. Searches by place (but not person) for these can be made on the TNA website, www.nationalarchives.gov.uk/e179.

There is a list of subsidy payers of Westminster for 1625–45 at the Society of Genealogists' Library. Civil War assessments can exist, too, there being detailed lists of taxpayers for 1641 and 1644 in the parishes making up the Hundred of Blackheath in *The Greenwich and Lewisham Antiquarian Society Transactions* of 1963.

Death Duties

From 1796, death duties became payable on estates as they passed from one owner on death to another. Until 1805, they only covered about a quarter of estates, but by 1857, all estates, unless valued at under £20, were included. If assets were valued at over £1,500, there would be a full reference. The surviving records are at TNA, IR26, with an index in IR27, and those from 1796–1811 are searchable by name online at TNA's website. Death duty registers show different information to wills; the latter show intent, these registers show what happened. They may also give information about the beneficiaries, addresses, the dates of birth, marriage and death of the deceased, family and other useful information. They also state in which diocesan court a will was proved.

As ever, tax records are more likely to exist for the wealthier members of society, but also serve as lists of most householders, except for the very poorest. The latter feature much less in these records than they do in others, such as the lists of those relieved with these rates and taxes, as mentioned in Chapter 3.

Chapter 11

LISTS OF PEOPLE

Family historians need lists of names in order to search through them to find their ancestors, and as much information as can be ascertained about them. Few such lists survive which can claim to be anything near universal; from 1841 to 1911 these would be the national censuses. There is nothing like this for our period, but there are some major listings which do exist, and hopefully your ancestors will appear on one or more of them.

Early Census Records

Readers may be aware that, although the national census began in 1801 and then for each ten years thereafter, excepting 1941, there was no requirement for anything but numbers before that of 1841. Thus for the genealogist it is the censuses of 1841 and onwards which are of use and this is often stated in books about family history. And yet that is not, happily, the whole story. There have been censuses throughout England since the sixteenth century, and these have included names.

Early censuses were created by some parishes, although it is not always known why they were created. Certainly there was no known central directive. Some are extremely detailed. That for Ealing in Middlesex of 1598 is arranged by household. It lists each resident, with age and occupation. One entry for one household tells us that Richard Rogers, husbandman, aged 50 is its head, then there are Elizabeth Rogers, his wife, aged 32, Elizabeth their daughter, aged 6, and Ellen their other daughter, aged 4. Also living with the family were Elizabeth Burgese, a servant, aged 20, and Nicholas Kinge, 36, and Robert Brown, aged 18, both described as 'servant husbandman'. There are also 'Easter books' which exist for the seventeenth and eighteenth centuries. These list all those in the parish who took communion at Easter, so will presumably exclude members of religious minorities such as Nonconformists, Catholics and Jews. Sometimes these books exist for a number of years. For example, there are Easter books for Ryton in Durham from 1593–1615.

There are hundreds of census returns for the years 1801–31 which list names, though this is still a minority of the whole. The returns in these

103

years were composed by parish officials, who sometimes recorded names. Often these were only the names of the heads of the household and the numbers in that household. An example from Ealing in 1811 tells that Edward Roberts was the householder and that one family dwelt there. It consisted of six males and five females; none was engaged in agriculture, but nine were involved in 'Trade, Manufacture or handicraft' and two fitted neither category. Yet all householders are included; unlike the lists of ratepayers, which only list those paying rates. In some cases, all the family are listed; occasionally ages are given. Those for Foxley, Norfolk, in 1831 list all names and birth dates are also included. The information is far less than in later censuses, but is invaluable in listing where someone was in given years.

1811 Ealing Census Ealing. Local History Library.

These census returns are usually found where the parish archives are held; in the county or borough record office. Some have been published and indexed by family history societies, so a quick search is possible. The best guide to what exists and its whereabouts is Jeremy Gibson and Mervyn Medlycott's *Local Census Listings, 1522–1930*.

Militia and Volunteer Forces

We have already surveyed sources for the regular forces of the Crown. Men have been occasionally armed and organized to supplement them since Anglo-Saxon times for home defence. These men were known as the fyrd and composed most of Harold's army at Hastings in 1066, yet we know nothing about individuals who served therein. In the sixteenth century the militia was deemed that force of men aged 16–60 summoned by the Lords Lieutenant of the counties in times of rebellion and feared invasion as ordered by the monarch. They would be armed with pikes, longbows and makeshift weaponry and formed into units, but would usually not serve beyond their county's borders and even then only for a very limited period. Musters of the militia were meant to be held every year for training, but these were often infrequent. Many were summoned at the time of the Spanish Armada in 1588. In 1662, there was new legislation, stating that propertied individuals had to supply a man for the militia. In 1757, the new Militia Act gave this responsibility to the parish, with men chosen by ballot, though those chosen could pay for a substitute.

There are a number of militia lists for the Tudor and Stuart periods. Some are held at TNA. These are lists of over 300 pikemen and musketeers of 1539. Another roll thirty years later lists 6,000 Londoners. Other rolls cover 1590–1601, giving names of hundreds of men, with details of their birthplaces and current parish. The LMA holds City muster rolls for a number of years between 1682 and 1724. There are two very useful guides to the location of militia records; J S W Gibson and A Dell, *Tudor and Stuart Muster Rolls* (1991). Muster Rolls should list the militiamen and their arms, as well as parish of residence and occupation. Some have been published, such as J Smith, *Men and Armour for Gloucestershire in 1608*, which includes almost 20,000 names.

Then there are the records of London's oldest military unit, if we except the Yeoman of the Guard. This is the Honourable Artillery Company, founded in 1537. Muster rolls exist from 1611–1862 and then onwards for officers only (the earlier rolls were lost during the Civil Wars). These give the names, ages, heights and ranks of those men who composed the Company. All men were volunteers and there are over 30,000 names on the rolls. These cannot be inspected by the public, but the Company's Archivist must be contacted with details of any individual for whom information is required. Lists, with details of men who formed the King's bodyguards, the Yeomen of the Guard, can be found at TNA.

There is a myth encouraged by standard texts and works on the militia that the institution was moribund between 1660 and 1757. This is not the case. They were called out to deal with public disorder as well as internal rebellion in the later seventeenth and eighteenth centuries. Crises in the seventeenth century such as the Venner revolt of 1661 and the Monmouth rebellion of 1685 (to name but two) led to their being summoned into action. After 1685, the next conflict in which large number of men were involved in military activity was during the Jacobite rebellions of 1715 and 1745. Although the militia were called out in 1715, relatively few records survive. One exception is for Berkshire, where there are lists of men from the county's four companies, but no further information is given. There are lists of militia officers, but not men, for other counties. Survival of lists from 1745 is rather better. Lists of men from the Cumberland and Westmorland Militia, differentiated between Horse and Foot, can be found in Rupert Jarvis, *The Jacobite Risings of 1715 and 1745* (1954). Durham's Dean and Chapter Archives list, in the Sharp MSS, the members of Durham's Horse Volunteers and York City Archives has lists of that city's volunteer forces. Yet in some cases only lists of officers survive, such as those of the Liverpool Blues, in the Shairp MSS at the Merseyside Maritime Museum, and in any case there is little else except names. Furthermore, in 1745, many noblemen chose to raise men in newly formed regiments of the regular army but no lists of these survive.

The New Militia of 1757 resulted in the constable of each parish drawing up lists of able-bodied men, with occupations, which were to be sent to the Lords Lieutenant of the county. Some occupations, such as clergymen, sailors and apprentices, were excused. These men might not be included in the constables' lists. Poverty and ill health were other reasons for exemptions. There would then be a ballot to decide who would serve. These lists provide the most comprehensive lists of adult men prior to the national censuses. J S W Gibson and M Medlycott, *Militia Rolls and Musters, 1757–1876* (1994) should be consulted on the whereabouts of such archives.

Then there were the French Revolutionary and Napoleonic Wars of 1793–1815. At the end of the eighteenth century, with heightened fears of an invasion from France, apart from the men in the army and Navy, many flocked to join militia, volunteer and yeomanry forces, as occurred more famously in 1940. It has been estimated that, at the end of 1803, there were 35,256 men in the London, Middlesex, Tower Hamlets and Westminster volunteer forces. In the following year, there were twenty-six units formed in Middlesex and twenty-three in London.

Although there are published Militia, Yeomanry and Volunteer Lists, produced annually for this period, only the officers are listed, with rank and date enlisted. We can learn that Thomas Clutterbuck was captain of the Great Stanmore company, that Richard Andrews was his lieutenant and Francis Schrafton the ensign, and that the first two joined on 18 August 1803 and the latter on 29 October 1803. The Spelthorne Legion was a regiment with thirty-eight officers. From 1804 the lists are indexed by name and place, and are arranged in alphabetical order by county. Yet, as before, there are no names of those who served as sergeants, corporals and privates. They were clearly not viewed as being important enough to merit inclusion as named individuals.

Some other institutions hold military archives for the late eighteenth and early nineteenth centuries. The LMA holds the enormous militia ballot for Westminster of 28,000 names. There are also held there discharge papers of 4,000 men who had seen active military and naval service and so were exempt from the usual requirement to be a Freeman in order to trade in the City. Some local authority archives have archives of military bodies; Bexley has militia pay lists for Bexley parish, 1803–1809, Chislehurst and Footscray, 1803–1805, and a muster roll for Crayford for 1803 and the total number of names in these is 500. Militia Attestation Rolls from 1806–1915 can be searched at findmy.past.com.

Following the defeat of Napoleon in 1815, other units were formed to deal with any home-grown revolutionary activity. These units were often cavalry, the yeomanry, made up of gentlemen and their servants, uniformed and armed. They had a bad reputation for poor discipline, as occurred at Peterloo in 1819 where several civilians were killed, but in fact few saw action. Lists of members can be found at county and borough record offices, though it is more common to find the names of officers rather than rank and file.

Lists of Loyalty

There were many periods of serious crisis for the state in the seventeenth and eighteenth centuries. Rebellion, conspiracy and invasion were all feared by the government, especially by those of the state's religious minorities at a time when it was thought that political and religious loyalty went hand in hand. Periodic fears about Catholics were especially frequent because, although relatively few in number, they might be sympathetic to Catholic powers hostile to Britain, notably France and Spain. So the government and its allies in local administration worked together to encourage manifestations of loyalty, among both allies and suspected enemies, and this activity created paperwork listing people.

One of the first examples is the Protestation Lists of 1642, drawn up when the country was on the brink of Civil War. Churchwardens and constables of each parish had to draw up lists of those adult men who would 'live and die for the true Protestant religion, the liberties and rights of subjects and the privileges of Parliament'. These lists enumerated the parish's Protestant men and the Catholic men; no more information is given. These surviving lists can be found in the House of Lords Record Office; there are some copies at the British Library Manuscripts Room. Some county and borough record offices have copies.

Jacobite threats resulted in other lists being drawn up from 1696 to 1745. Following an assassination plot against William III in 1696, lists of London men who took the oath of allegiance to the reigning monarch were drawn up and can be found at TNA (ref. C214/9). Association Rolls for 1696 can be seen on Origins.net. In 1745 those in Middlesex who supported George II and paid for military support appended their names and sums promised to a list (found at the Bodleian Library). There were other lists of Catholics drawn up at other times, known as the Recusant Rolls of 1592–1691, listing those who did not attend Anglican service and so were fined (located at TNA, E376–7) and during 1778–1857 (TNA again, E169/79–83). County record offices often hold lists created at this time, though those listed are usually among the more affluent in society and mostly men.

Catholics and Nonconformists were often suspected of disloyalty towards the state, especially during times of crisis, such as war and rebellion. Because of this, the state took a great, if occasional, interest in their affairs and so records were created about them and their property. Many lists of individuals (mostly adult males) are held at TNA. Pipe Rolls and Recusancy Rolls which exist at TNA (E372, 376, 377) list Catholics from 1581–1691. Sometimes, parish officials were requested to make returns of Catholics within their parish; several occurred in the early seventeenth century (located in TNA, SP 16/495), one was made in 1708 (TNA, SP 34/26) and others later in the century, and there is a published *Returns of Papists, 1767: Dioceses of England and Wales except Chester* (1989). Another published list is the Cosin's list, *The Names of Roman Catholics, Non Jurors and others who refus'd to take the Oaths* (1862). G L Turner's *Original Records of Early Nonconformity under Persecution and Indulgence* lists many Dissenters, with names and addresses and denominations, taken from numerous sources. The Association Oath of 1696 to William III resulted in lists of London Dissenters (C214/9) and Baptist ministers in London (C213/170). Quaker lawyers made similar declarations in 1831–42 (E3 and CP10). Likewise, there are lists of Catholic lawyers, 1790–1836 at TNA (CP10, C217/180/5) and for 1830–75 (E3). More general oaths of allegiance are located at TNA (E169/79–83), which cover 1778–1857, giving names and addresses. Quarter session indictments often list Dissenters and Catholics who did not attend the services at the Anglican parish church and these people were named and fined, especially in the sixteenth and seventeenth century.

Although there was less persecution after 1689, it still occurred periodically, especially for Catholics who were often assumed to be in league with the exiled Catholic Stuart pretenders. This resulted in Catholics coming under the state's attention. For example, in George I's reign, all Catholic property owners had their estates detailed by officials for the government (records existing at TNA, E174). Details of Catholic estates for 1625–84 are located at TNA, E351/414–52.

Nonconformist clergy had to have their premises licensed for worship after 1688. These requests are usually found with the quarter sessions at the county record office in question, giving details of the minister and the location of the chapel. Catholic priests had to do likewise, after 1791, and letters by all these men can be found at the LMA. Close Rolls at TNA give information about deeds referring to use of land and property by Nonconformists (C54 and, from 1902, J18). These have been indexed and so are relatively easy to use.

It was not only Catholics who appear on lists during this time. In 1745 there were many who wished to assert their loyalty to George II. Many counties formed volunteer units to assist the regular troops and to counter any possible local Jacobite action. To pay for these forces, voluntary subscriptions were called for. This led to lists of subscribers being drawn up, together with sums of money promised. Many still exist. There are lists for Essex, Hampshire, Hertfordshire, Hull, Middlesex, Scarborough, York and Yorkshire, among others. Some of these have been published, some exist at the county record office in question and those for Yorkshire are reproduced in Jonathan Oates's *Responses in North East England to the Jacobite Rebellions of 1715 and 1745*. These lists are sometimes in alphabetical order. Nobility, gentry and clergy appear disproportionately in these lists, as they had most to lose from a defeat of the religious and political status quo, as well as having more spare money. Yet many less affluent people are also listed, albeit paying smaller sums.

Another rebellion against the Crown which led to a mass of loyalist addresses was that in the American colonies in 1775. From September 1775 to March 1776, addresses, with lists of those who signed them, were published in *The London Gazette* newspaper. These can be seen at TNA, the British Library and at the British Library Newspaper Library at Colindale. Although these petitions don't give any personal information, they are useful for two reasons. First, they give an indication as to an individual's politics and secondly they show where he was living at that time.

Other Lists

There are many other lists of people drawn up through the centuries for a myriad of different reasons. Two examples are two valuable works by the Camden Society (published in 1847 and 1848 respectively) which include extensive lists of people: 'The Diary of Henry Maclyn', a very busy undertaker, for 1550–63, which lists those he buried, and 'The Obituary of Richard Smyth', covering 1627–75, with much biographical information about the middling people of the capital. Both are indexed. As with other Camden Society publications, they can be viewed at TNA.

Friendly Societies and Masonic Lodges

These groups were prominent in the eighteenth and nineteenth centuries and promoted brotherhood among members (and sisterhood for the former). During the 1790s, with fears about revolution spreading from France, the government ordered that societies register themselves with the JPs. This became annual and resulted in lists of names of members being created. These can be found, when they survive, at county record offices.

Freemen's Rolls

For urban residents, it was important that a man was admitted to the freedom of the city. This allowed him to practise his craft or trade, and to vote. Freedom was achieved on the completion of apprenticeship, by following a father's trade or could be granted by the order of the mayor and corporation. Names were recorded on an annual basis, from the thirteenth century onwards, though these are less useful from the eighteenth. They can be found at county or borough record offices. Some have been published. They can note name, date of admission, name and occupation of father or name and occupation of master, depending on how admission was gained. Many townsmen were never freemen, of course, and these include servants, apprentices and labourers. Women and children were excluded.

A degree of luck will determine whether the types of lists mentioned here will be of use to you. Many have been published by county record societies and have been indexed. They should be easily available at the appropriate county record offices and libraries, and there is a large national collection at TNA's library.

Chapter 12

MISCELLANEOUS SOURCES

It is worth remembering that almost any document can contain information relevant to your research. Clearly, those documents which cover the period and place which coincides with your ancestor's whereabouts may be very rewarding.

Personal accounts, such as diaries, memoirs and memoranda books, even if they were not written by your ancestor, are one example. If your ancestor lived in East Hoathley in Sussex between 1754 and 1765, it would be worth reading the diary of Thomas Turner, a shopkeeper there, and whose diary extracts were published in 1984 (a copy of the complete diary is at the Bodleian Library, and the original is in the USA). Turner made many references to fellow parishioners who he came into contact with, either as fellow parish officers, customers of his shop, friends, family and neighbours. Not all these are flattering. He wrote of one Jeremiah French thus: 'quite stupid through drinking', he 'would never willingly be without a dram of gin in his hand'. Even if your ancestor was not mentioned there, the diary gives a firsthand account of what it was like to live in that village at that time. There are many other diaries of course, those of John Evelyn, Samuel Pepys and the Revd James Woodforde being other well-known ones. These have all been published and are often well indexed by name, so searching for an ancestor is straightforward. Published correspondence, such as that of Horace Walpole (1717–97), which has been indexed by name, can be very useful.

Immigration

Most people tend to think of those people who have arrived since 1945 when the word immigration is mentioned. Yet it should be remembered that many people will have ancestors who arrived into England in previous centuries. Many came in search of work, such as the Irish, from the Middle Ages onwards. Following the Reformation of the sixteenth century, Protestants arrived in England, fleeing religious persecution in Catholic France or Germany. Jews were allowed to resettle in England in the 1650s, following one of Cromwell's rare liberal pieces of legislation.

Revolution in France in 1789 led to many Frenchmen journeying to England to escape the Terror with their lives.

Most of those arriving in Britain before the nineteenth century were from the European Continent. These were French Huguenots and German Protestants who were fleeing religious tyranny from their home Catholic states. The former are well known, in part because of the work of the Huguenot Society, in publishing and indexing relevant records. *Returns of Aliens in London, 1523–1625* is a published source, giving names of foreigners in the capital and the taxes paid by them (alien was a term for a foreigner). Then there were three surveys of aliens living in London, two in 1571 and one in 1618. These can be viewed at TNA in SP12/82 and 84 and in SP14/102. Huguenots in London tended to settle in Spitalfields and

Statue of William III. Paul Lang's collection.

Soho. The Huguenot Society (www.huguenotsociety.org.uk) can be contacted directly about Huguenot ancestors (for a fee), or you can see the published documents at TNA or Guildhall Libraries. Palatine (German) refugees in London can be found in TNA, T 1/119, giving names and numbers of dependants.

Other sources include the indexes to the Calendars to State Papers Domestic (1509–1704) at TNA, and also the Calendars to Treasury Papers; again available at TNA and the British Library. Passes for incoming people in the eighteenth century were issued by the Secretaries of State, and noted in SP44/386–411 for 1697–1784 and FO366/544 for 1748–94. There are some indexes to these; in the forementioned State Papers calendars, up to 1704, then in the Calendar of Home Office Papers, 1760–75. The political turmoil caused by the French Revolution in 1789 led to a new surge of refugees from France, this time escaping political, not religious terror. Some returns to the Aliens' Office for 1810–11 survive at FO83/21–2. Newcomers, from 1793–1836, were subject to the Aliens Act of the former year, but very few records survive. Newcomers had to register with the justices of the peace, giving name, address, rank and occupation. This information was sent in the form of certificates to the Home Office. After 1826, such records are found in HO2, and are indexed up to 1849 in HO5/25–32. Alien arrivals for 1810–11 and 1826–69 can be searched online by name at ancestry.co.uk .

The LMA has a few records relating to the registration of aliens for the late eighteenth century. There are accounts for aliens in Middlesex completed and signed for a number of northern Middlesex parishes for 1797, and returns made by overseers or householders for a few other parishes in Middlesex and Westminster. These aliens include French, Italians and Germans. One example is of a house in the parish of St Anne's, where it was noted, 'Charles Chevalier de Beaumont, alien, has taken the house no. 43 Gerrard Street . . . on the 5th of October, 1797'. Living with him were four named lodgers, all French, and 'belonging to the opera house'. These are listed under MR/A for Middlesex and WR/A for Westminster.

Naturalization

Many immigrants became legally British subjects by either receiving letters of denization or, in later centuries, by being naturalized. This meant that they had all the privileges of natural born Britons, which included voting rights. Letters of denizen exist from the sixteenth century, when about 7,000 were granted. A number of volumes of the Huguenot Society cover the centuries prior to 1800. These are vol. 8, *Letters of Denization and Acts of Naturalisation for Aliens in England, 1509–1603*, vol. 18, for 1603–1700, and vol. 27, covering 1701–1800. The latter two volumes also cover Ireland.

Emigration and Foreign Travel

Many people have had to travel overseas in centuries past. Usually a licence was required. Certainly from the sixteenth century to 1677, the government issued licences to do so. These can be found at TNA, E157. They include those given to soldiers serving in the Low Countries, people travelling to Europe and to the colonies. Passports from 1791 onwards are also held there, at FO610. Passenger lists survive for those travelling from Bristol to the American colonies from 1654–79 at Bristol Record Office.

Charities

From the sixteenth century wealthy individuals left sums of money to be invested in property or stock in order that an income be created to pay for a charitable purpose. This might be educational or to relieve poverty. Usually a number of trustees would administer these funds and disbursements. However, recipients of such sums are rarely mentioned. Rather it is the benefactors and trustees' names which are most likely to be found in such documentation.

Coroners

The office of coroner has existed in England since 1194, but their functions have varied over the centuries. The medieval coroner was usually a knight and he dealt with felons' appeals, outlawry, felons' abjurations as well as holding inquests on sudden or suspicious deaths. By 1487 only the latter function remained. After 1660 they dealt with treasure trove.

Although coroners' records survive from the thirteenth century onwards, their existence for the early centuries is patchy. Most medieval ones are held at TNA in record series JUST2. Later coroners' records for London and Middlesex are also held here, at KB9 (1485–1675) and KB10 (post-1675) and for other counties in KB11.

Patent Rolls

The Court of Chancery issued letters from 1201 to 1946. Copies are held at TNA. They include grants to individuals and corporations and refer to lands, privileges, licences and denization. There are printed calendars at TNA, for 1216–1582 and 1584–7. Those for 1509–47 are in the Calendars of State Papers for the reign of Henry VIII.

Hospitals

There were a number of hospitals in the cities of medieval and early modern England, and especially in London, with further establishments being founded in the eighteenth century. Few relevant documents survive from these times, however. The British Lying In Hospital catered for expectant mothers, especially those whose husbands were in the armed forces, but entrants had to have a sponsor. For the period 1749–1868, there are the hospital's admission registers, which list the parents' names, father's occupation, mother's age, place of settlement, expected date of delivery, date of admission and birth, dates of discharge or death, and name of recommender. The archives, which list 42,008 admissions, are to be found at TNA, RG8/52–61.

Another London hospital was Thomas Coram's Foundling Hospital of 1741, to look after infants which would otherwise be abandoned. From 1760, parents could petition for their babies to be placed here. Baptism and burial registers are at TNA, RG4/4396 and 4328. Apprenticeship records are at the London Metropolitan Archives, as are the aforesaid petitions.

Seals

Individuals often appended documents with their personal seal, made of wax and bearing an image and wording about the edge. These were usually round, but could be oval in the case of clergy and ladies. The seals for the Duchy of Lancaster (several thousand) have been made available online from the thirteenth to the eighteenth centuries and can be searched by name on TNA's website.

Tontines and Annuities

The former were named after Tonti, an Italian banker, in the seventeenth century, and was a method of the government raising money and of investors securing an income. Basically people paid into the funds and reaped an annual income from it. The income ceased at the death of the nominee chosen by the fund holder (usually a young child was chosen), but as nominees died off, their share was returned to the fund, thus ensuring a greater yield for the remainder. When the last nominee died the capital was returned to the government. There were three English tontines: in 1693, 1766 and 1789. About 15,000 people participated in it; usually the better off. Archives pertaining to these tontines can be found at TNA, NDO1–2. There are indexes and information in these archives refers to the participants and their nominees.

Annuities paid out an income for life after an initial investment, but the amount received did not increase as others died off. The archives are in the source listed above. Often these were purchased by those who wished to cease their current occupation and had a lump sum to invest to provide them with a future income.

There were also private tontines, such as the British Tontine of 1792. Its records were taken by the Chancery Courts during a dispute and can be found in TNA, C114/166–8. These volumes list the tontine's subscribers.

Heraldry

Coats of arms belong to specific individuals and their heirs usually through the male line, not to everyone who shares that surname, and date from the twelfth century. The system of coats of arms has been policed since the Middle Ages by Officers of Arms and Heralds, and now by the College of Arms. These officials have created records which may lead you to another avenue in your research.

There are several sources which you can use. First, is to contact the College of Arms at Queen Victoria Street, London EC4V 4BT. However their resources are closed to the public and you will need to pay them for research. Or you could try the Heraldry Society at PO Box 722, Guilford, Surrey GU3 3ZX, whose library is open to fee-paying members. Or you could try investigating armorials. These are alphabetical lists of those eligible to bear coats of arms, such as Burke's *The General Armory of England, Scotland, Ireland and Wales*, containing tens of thousands of names.

Coat of arms of William Whitehead, Saffron Waldon. Author's collection.

116

The Herald's Visitations of 1530–1684 have been published on a county by county basis by the Harleian Society in over 100 volumes. They have been indexed and can be located at large libraries and record offices. These were inspections undertaken a regular intervals by the heralds to ascertain and verify those who had the right to bear a coat of arms. In order to do so, they had to check the genealogy of those who claimed to bear such arms. Therefore the heralds would amass a number of pedigrees, which include family trees stretching back centuries.

Existing Pedigrees

It is possible that someone may already have researched part of your family tree. Before the late twentieth-century enthusiasm for genealogy, there were previous phases of history in which the pastime was popular, albeit for small sections of society. Many wanted to prove their descent from aristocracy or royalty. The results of their labours have often been deposited in archives and libraries. There are many at the British Library (see www.bl.uk/catalogues/manuscripts.html), the College of Arms and the Society of Genealogists' Library. Not all were manuscripts, as many have been published in works such as Burke's and Debrett's as previously described, but Victoria County History volumes (see Bibliography) some-times contain pedigrees. Volumes on the descendants of medieval monarchs include *The Plantagenet Roll of the Blood Royal* (1928), listing 50,000 names and *The Royal Bastards of Medieval England* (1986).

The temptation is, of course, to try and link these trees to your own and to save yourself a lot of work. However it is essential to check the informa-tion provided, as earlier researchers may have erred by optimism. As with every piece of non-primary evidence, use it as a tool, but do not depend on it unquestioningly.

General Points

It is also worth finding out about what was going on around your ances-tors in their locality in the past, or in the places that they visited during their lifetime, perhaps as part of their career. There are many local history books available for sale in shops or for loan from libraries, and there are very few places for which there is no published history. These may be great events of national importance or lesser events of local significance. For example if your ancestors lived in the Lancashire towns of Preston, Lancaster or Manchester in November or December 1745, they would probably have witnessed the Jacobite army marching through their streets. There may have been a battle near or in the town or village – St Albans witnessed two in the 1450s. Or on a lesser level, a notable personality may have lived locally; Henry Fielding resided in the Middlesex village of

Ealing in 1753–4, for example. Or if your ancestor was in the army or navy, you could check regimental or naval histories to find out which campaigns and battles they were involved in. It is usually very difficult, if not impossible, to know what your ancestor felt or did about these. Speculation is best avoided. However, an awareness of the context of your ancestors' lives is well worth acquiring.

Published accounts by travellers such as Celia Fiennes in the late seventeenth century, Daniel Defoe in the early eighteenth or Viscount Torrington in the late eighteenth all give firsthand impressions of villages and towns in England in these periods. The latter described Knutsford in Cheshire, thus: 'a clean, well-built, well-placed town where the cotton trade brings plenty'. On the other hand, he writes scathingly of the dirty town of Cambridge, only relieved by the magnificence of King's College chapel, whereas Celia Fiennes condemns the smoking of tobacco pipes by women and children in a West Country inn and Defoe praises the tolerance shown to Catholics in Durham.

Histories of the village or town where your ancestor lived should also be consulted. Maps and pictures of the same can often be located in the county or borough record office where your ancestor lived. These should give an additional insight into your ancestor's life. On a more mundane level, if your ancestor worked on the land, the history might tell which were the major crops or livestock which were farmed there. Genealogy shouldn't restrict itself to names and dates, but also to the environment that your ancestor lived in – certainly a world far removed from our own.

To recap, check any relevant records for a district for the period that your ancestor resided in it. Even if a reference to the family is not made therein, you will have learnt about the place where they lived and some of the events and people that they may have been influenced by.

Seals belonging to medieval labourers. Paul Lang's collection.

Chapter 13

PLACES TO VISIT

There are over 1,000 institutions which hold archives in England, to which access is permitted. It is, of course, impossible to list them all. However, it is worth discussing the most important and outlining others.

For most of these places entry is by reader's ticket. These are issued freely, but you will need to bring two proofs of identity. A passport and driving licence, or a recent utility bill, are among the forms of identity accepted. Once inside, coats and bags must be left in lockers and pencils only are allowed to take notes, unless you have a laptop. Archives and other material can usually be ordered in advance of a visit, but only a limited amount. Most of what you see can be copied for personal use by photography or photocopying, but always check first. Fragile material has to be safeguarded so copying may not be allowed.

Most are open five or six days a week, with at least one evening opening, but never assume; some are not. Always contact these places in advance of any intended visit to avoid disappointment.

If you cannot visit in person, you may need to consider paying someone else to do this for you. Never expect these institutions' paid staff to undertake much research for you. They have many other tasks, but they should be able to tell you what their institution holds and may be able to undertake a short search for you for free. However, many places now charge for any searching.

All of these places will have websites which should state at least their major holdings. Catalogues may also be available online to search, and there may even be documents online, as is the case with TNA. Some of these documents can be viewed online for free, or at least searched via the indexes. Payment may be required for the full text of documents, however.

Over the centuries, and especially in the last 100 years, there have been many amalgamations and alterations in local government. These affect the location of centuries-old archives. You should consult the archives of the current local authority whose boundaries include those districts that you are interested in. So, for the archives of Twickenham or Teddington, for which there is now no local authority with those names, you would need to consult the Local Studies Centre of Richmond, the borough of which these are now part. Yet you would also need to visit the London Metropolitan Aechives as these places were once administratively part of Middlesex. Yorkshire's boundaries have changed so much that some former parishes of that county have their archives stored in record offices outside the county (Nottinghamshire and Lancashire, to name but two).

The National Archives

Ruskin Avenue, Kew, Surrey TW9 (tel. 020 8876 3444); car park (must be booked in advance), nearest tube station Kew
Probably the single most important place for family historians. Formed in 1841 as the Public Record Office in Chancery Lane, it transferred entirely to a new site at Kew in 1997 and in 2002 was renamed The National Archives. It is the record office to the government of the United Kingdom and so holds the archives of government departments such as the Home Office, the Foreign Office and the War Office, to name but three.

There is free electronic access to the digitized sources which elsewhere would require payment. These include the PCC Wills. There is also an extremely good library. This includes most of the county record society publications, especially useful for they contain indexed transcripts of many key sources, such as oaths of loyalty, quarter session records, militia lists, letters and diaries. There are the Calendars of State Papers, 1509–1704, and Calendars of Treasury Papers and Books up to 1745.

Among the archives are those of the regular army (excepting the Guards) prior to 1921, and the Royal Navy and Royal Marines. There are assize records, archives relating to transportation, and archives of the Metropolitan Police, the Yeomen of the Guard and of the Bow Street Runners. Manorial and taxation records can also be located here. It is a veritable treasure trove for family historians. You can order items in advance via the website if you already have a ticket.

TNA has a vast amount of catalogue records and online documents available on their website, along with numerous research guides to their collections. The same research guides are available in paper copies on site. Below are the parts of the website relevant to the pre-1837 period.

http://www.nationalarchives.gov.uk/documentsonline/
Duchy of Lancashire Seals, 12th–18th century
Seamen's Wills, 1786–1882
Death Duty Registers, 1796–1811
PCC Wills, 1383–1858
Doomsday Book
Ancient Petitions, 13th–17th century
Equity Pleadings, 1625–1714

The British Library Newspaper Library

Colindale Avenue, London NW9 5HE (tel. 020 7412 7353); www.bl.uk/collectionsnewspapers.html; nearest tube Colindale (Northern Line)

Local and national newspapers from the early eighteenth century onwards can be seen here. Up to four items can be ordered in advance. Some of these newspapers are on microfilm but occasionally you will see the originals in bound volumes. The collection is by no means comprehensive. Many county newspapers for the eighteenth century are lacking, for example. Again, checking their website in advance is highly recommended.

The British Library

96 Euston Road, London NW1 2DB (tel. 0870 444 1500); www.bl.uk

This was created in 1973 from an amalgamation of several libraries. It holds the single largest collection of books in the UK. Access is by reader's ticket. There are several collections of special interest to the family historian. The Burney Collection of eighteenth-century newspapers can be viewed here on microfilm. These are all national newspapers such as *The London Gazette* and *The Daily Courant*. There are also a few seventeenth-century titles (accessible in the Rare Books Reading Room). The India Office Library (tel. 020 7412 7873, www.bl.uk/collections/orientalandindian.html) holds the archives of the East India Company. Then there is the manuscript collection. The Cotton and Harleian collections there contain much relevant to medieval studies, and these can be searched by using the ten-volume index. There is also an extensive collection of maps and the recordings of the British Sound Archive. Finally, there are the books, many of which are held off site at Boston Spa, and these can be searched for and ordered on the online catalogue. The British Library is a copyright library, so has in theory a copy of all books published in the UK.

The Guildhall Library

Aldermanbury, London EC2P 2EJ; nearest tube station, Bank

This holds some archival sources, such as watermen's records and insurance records, and is also a rich source of printed books. Although the collection concentrates on London's history, the extensive collection of county and town directories is remarkable. These have to be ordered, but do not take long to arrive and no reader's ticket is needed.

*Guildhall
Library, London,*
Paul Lang's
collection.

The Society of Genealogists' Library

14 Charterhouse Buildings, Goswell Road, London EC1M 7BA (tel. 020 7251 8799); www.sog.org.uk
Not an archive centre, but a vast private collection of copies of genealogical research sources, including parish registers from throughout the country. A daily fee is payable, unless one becomes a member and pays an annual subscription (worth doing if you live in or near London but have to consult copies of material of which the originals are held elsewhere). There is a regular series of lectures, aimed at both beginners and more experienced researchers. These often focus on particular types of ancestor, such as seamen, criminals or paupers. Members pay reduced rates for these events.

The Borthwick Institute

University of York, Heslington YO10 5DD (tel. 01904 321166); www.york.ac.uk/borthwick
Although this is part of the University of York, it is unique in being the only university archive which is also the diocesan record office. Apart from the PCY wills, as well as those for the other ecclesiastical courts in the diocese, there are ecclesiastical court records, visitation records and bishops' transcripts, and an immense quantity of parish archives, not just for York, but from all the ridings of Yorkshire, although many parish archives for the county can be found in the county's other record offices.

County Record Offices

These began in the 1920s; Bedfordshire Record Office being one of the first. Legislation in the 1950s and 1960s allowed county councils to spend money on acquiring, preserving and making their archives accessible. The core of these collections is the archives of the county council and its predecessor bodies, but they also collect a wide variety of other archives pertaining to their county. More and more counties formed their own archive services, so by the 1970s all counties possessed one, staffed with professionally qualified archivists.

It is impossible to categorize each county record office. They reflect the post-1974 county boundaries; so the West Riding has been divided into West and South Yorkshire. Some counties have a single record office located in the county town, such as that at Chelmsford, which covers Essex. Some will have a main office and a subsidiary office, as in the case of Hampshire, with Winchester being the headquarters and Southampton having a branch. West Yorkshire has five offices: Wakefield is the centre, with branches in Bradford, Halifax, Huddersfield and Leeds. The metropolitan districts of Greater Manchester and Birmingham have myriad record offices, each serving a district council which makes up the metropolitan area.

They house the county's principal administrative archives, such as those of the quarter sessions and the Lords Lieutenant. Estate records often survive, with the Althorp archives being housed at Northamptonshire county record office for example, or Wentworth-Woodhouse at Sheffield Archives. Family papers can be located here, too. If the county record office is also the diocesan record office, as most are outside Yorkshire, diocesan records will be here. In any case, parish archives are almost certainly here. Manorial records for manors in the county are often located here, too. There will also be a good collection of relevant county record society volumes and a library of reference works.

The largest is the London Metropolitan Archives, which is an

123

amalgamation of the Middlesex and London County Council record offices and that of the Corporation of London Record Office. It has archives of London and Middlesex wide bodies, some Jewish archives and personnel records of the City of London Police. As with TNA, they have a large number of research guides pertaining to their archives (the same can be said on a lesser scale of most county record offices).

Borough Record Offices

These are far smaller establishments than those of the counties, in terms of both material held and staffing. Where the borough is part of a county, there will usually be overlap in holdings copies of such material. Archives of the corporation will be found here; York City Archives hold the records of York Corporation, for instance. These can include minute books, treasurers' accounts, militia lists, lists of councillors and aldermen and city officials.

University Libraries

The libraries of the medieval colleges of Oxford and Cambridge are the oldest surviving libraries in the country. They hold many valuable archival collections, often of the colleges themselves, so expect to find information of former masters and scholars, possibly college servants, too. These archives also include the manorial records of the manors which the colleges held. For instance, the manor court rolls for Ruislip, Middlesex, are held in the library of King's College, Cambridge. They hold all kinds of unexpected treasures. The Bodleian Library (Broad Street, Oxford OX1 3BG, tel. 01865 277158, www.bodley.ox.ac.uk), founded in 1598, holds copies of eighteenth-century Newcastle newspapers, for example, as well as the diaries of a female Nantwich Dissenter for the early eighteenth century. Wills proved at the Chancellor of Oxford's court are also held here. Durham University Dean and Chapter Library has the Sharp Manuscripts, the collection of an ecclesiastical antiquary. However, the more recent universities tend to lack such archives and concentrate on modern records. Access to university archives is not a general right, and special application must be made, often via a letter of introduction; and expect to pay a fee.

Local History Libraries

These are often to be found in a county's or a borough's central library. They tend to hold copies of the county's newspaper from the eighteenth century onwards, maps and pictures of the locality, as well as copies of primary material held elsewhere, such as parish registers on microfilm.

They tend not to hold original archival material, but exceptions to this rule can sometimes be found. Leeds Local and Family History Library holds the manuscript Memorandum Book of John Lucas, 1712–50, for instance.

Libraries

There have been libraries in England since the Middle Ages. Merton College's library dates from the thirteenth century and is thought to be the oldest one still in use. However public libraries date from the Victorian period and by 1914 there were few places which lacked one. They received much of their stock in the early decades from donations. Some of these were items of local and family history significance. They are often housed in the reference section unless they have been moved elsewhere. Libraries will almost always have books about how to research your family history, as well as books about local history which can be borrowed.

Cathedral Archives

The Church has always kept records. Many of these are now held in diocesan record offices, but cathedrals often maintain their own small repositories, too. York Minster, St Paul's Cathedral, Canterbury Cathedral and Westminster Abbey are all examples of these. Advance booking is

British Library, 2011. Author.

essential as only a very small number of researchers, sometimes only two or three, can be accommodated at any one time.

Lambeth Palace Library (London SE1 7JU, tel. 020 7898 1400, www.lambethpalacelibrary.org), founded in 1610, houses additional archives of the archbishopric of Canterbury. These include the wills of the Court of Arches and a number from the province's peculiars, and marriage licences.

Specialist Repositories

Many organizations have founded their own archive service of records, geared to suit their own organization as well as researchers in general. These are often privately held archives so a fee may be charged for access. For instance, the Duke of Devonshire's archives are to be found in his home, Chatsworth House in Derbyshire, and these can usually be accessed by arrangement and for a daily fee.

Museums

There have been museums in England for centuries. Elias Ashmole's at Oxford is one of the oldest, dating to the late seventeenth century, and now known as the Ashmolean. There are two main types of museum; those which are national in character, such as the National Army Museum and the National Maritime Museum, both in London, and the local museums which proliferate in the counties and cities of England. Some focus on the history of a county or town, and there are very many of these. Traditionally they focused on archaeology but now tend to concentrate on social and economic history of more recent centuries. They are increasingly user-friendly and many cater for children, too. Some museums are in historic houses and some focus on a particular event or individual or group of people. They vary greatly in size and facilities, ranging from small village museums run by volunteers to large museums which have programmes of lectures and educational features. Some may have libraries and research facilities. Many hold regular special exhibitions. Remember that what is on display is only a small proportion of the artefacts which the museum holds. Most artefacts will be held in storage, either on or off site. It may be worth contacting a museum in advance of a visit, in order to arrange to see any of this material which may be of particular interest to you.

Some museums are out of doors. There are museums such as the Chiltern Open Air Museum in Buckinghamshire or the Beamish Museum in Durham, which are collections of fairly ordinary dwellings and work-places in order to show how many rural people lived. At the other end of the scale are the country houses owned by the National Trust and English Heritage, which indicate how the gentry lived. There are also castles and a few battlefield museums on the site of past conflicts, such as Bosworth and Hastings. Many of these feature re-enactments of battles or other activities.

Most of these places will have a bookshop, which will probably also sell guides to specific aspects of family history. There may be other relevant matter, such as copies of old maps, postcards, perhaps even CDs or DVDs. Many will have a cafe, or at least places to eat a packed lunch.

Don't forget the myriad family history societies which exist in every county. The county or borough record office should be able to supply their contact details; otherwise try an internet search. These groups of like-minded enthusiasts hold regular meetings and talks by experts on aspects of family history. They produce regular newsletters and journals, which often include lists of ancestors' surnames which members are interested in, as well as general news about local family history.

Principal Websites

All these three subscription websites (i.e. pay to view) contain indexes to the civil registration records and to the census, from 1841. They also have the following, sometimes overlapping, features.

Ancestry.co.uk

London and Middlesex Parish Registers, 1538–20th century
Alien Arrivals, 1810–11, 1826–69
Alien Entry Books, 1794–1931
Extracted parish registers (various)
Andrew's newspaper index cards, 1790–1976
London Nonconformist registers, 1694–1921
Royal Navy officers, 1660–1815
Pallot's baptism and marriages register indexes, 1780–1837
Archdeaconry probate indexes (various)
Waterloo Medal Roll
Naval medal roll, 1793–1972
Military medals roll, 1793–1949
Criminal registers, 1791–1892
Various school and university rolls

www.Origins.net

National Wills Index (pre-1858)
Marriage Indexes (Surrey), 1500–1846
Marriage Indexes (Dorset), 1538–1856
Marriage indexes (London), 1538–1837

127

York Marriage Bonds indexes, 1613–1839
Association Rolls, 1696
City of London Burials, 1781–1904
Charles I Chancery Index, 1625–1649
Inheritance Disputes, 1574–1914
London Consistory Court deputations index, 1700–1713
London apprenticeships abstracts, 1442–1850

www.Findmypast.co.uk

British Army Service records, 1760–1913
Waterloo Medal Roll
Armed forces baptisms, 1761–2005
Armed forces marriages, 1796–2005
Armed forces burials
Miscellany military rolls, 1656–1888
Civil Service Evidences of Age, 1752–1948
Trinity House Calendars, 1787–1854
Apprentices, 1710–1774
Boyd's Inhabitants of London, 1700–1846
National Burial Index
Memorial Inscriptions
City of London Burials
Faculty Office Marriage Licence Allegations, 1701–1850
Vicar General Marriage Licences, 1694–1850
Boyd's London Burials, 1538–1872
Boyd's London, Marriages, 1538–1840
Boyd's London, Miscellany, 1538–1775
Militia Attestation Rolls, 1806–1915

Bear in mind that the content of these websites is constantly being updated, so do keep a watch out for what is on offer therein.

CONCLUSION

Hopefully this book has given the reader useful information in their search for their ancestors beyond the census and civil registration of the early nineteenth century. The main point to be emphasized is that, even more so than with the later period, it is essential to work back a generation at a time. This is to ensure that the people you are working on are the correct ones. As with all family history, luck plays its part. To quote Napoleon, don't tell me if he is a good general, just tell me if he is lucky! Having propertied ancestors also helps, as does having an ancestor who was in a profession for which archives are held. Of course, having criminal or pauper ancestors is not a disaster, for these people leave archives behind them, too. For those whose ancestors are neither, parish records and manorial records are probably the best single sources of recorded names.

Another good first step is to use the electronic sources available. TNA's website is a mine of information. The catalogue can be searched online, as can the index to the Prerogative Court of Canterbury's wills. The website Access to Archives (a2a) is another significant resource for it covers all deposited archives in the UK and can be searched online. The IGI is another online source. Ancestry.co.uk has London/Middlesex parish registers available, and both Origins.net and Findmypast.co.uk are other valuable tools for beginning your research. However much information you gain from these sources, you may well need to return to them with additional queries as you uncover more material from elsewhere.

Yet you will have to visit record offices and libraries and conduct research in the traditional manner, turning pages and sifting through parchment. Family research prior to 1837 is less easy than that for more recent times. However it is not impossible, and the assistance given here will hopefully help. Remember that each piece of information is not only important itself but can provide a clue to further information sources, just like a jigsaw puzzle.

Appendix 1

PALAEOGRAPHY AND LATIN FOR FAMILY HISTORIANS

There are two apparent difficulties facing family historians when venturing beyond 1837. One is that the handwriting is very different to our own. Almost all documents are manuscript, i.e. handwritten. Over the centuries, handwriting has changed considerably. Both the size and shape of letters, as well as the spelling, varied and is unlike our own. Furthermore, the language used is often Latin, especially in legal documents, up to 1733. And even then, this is not the Classical Latin as used by the Romans or in the few schools where the language is still taught. Rather it is a bastardized form. Spelling can be erratic as abbreviations are commonly used and proper nouns are far removed in spelling from our own period. Numbers are often expressed as Roman numerals.

Yet the researcher should not despair. There are some very useful guides. Eileen Gooder's *Latin for Local Historians* is one. It takes the reader through various documents which a family historian might encounter, and gives examples on which a beginner should work prior to attempting a 'real' manuscript. The Borthwick Institute (referred to in Chapter 13) sells a number of Borthwick Wallets which include further examples of copies of different forms of document which a researcher is likely to encounter. There is also a very useful guide on TNA website. It gives useful advice and also ten examples of handwriting which the reader is invited to transcribe as practice before 'real' documents are attempted, beginning with the least difficult and progressing in difficulty as the reader grows in confidence.

Possession of the guides mentioned above are recommended. So, too, are medieval Latin word lists, such as E McLaughlin, *Simple Latin for Family Historians* (1999) and J Morris, *A Latin Glossary for Family and Local Historians* (1989), for they concentrate on the words most likely to be found in the documents you will be examining.

Some handwriting is very good indeed. In the eighteenth and nineteenth century formal documents, such as quarter session order books, were written in a very clear hand. And, as we shall note in the next appendix, many medieval documents have already been calendared so can be seen without recourse to the originals. Most researchers, having dealt with post-1831 census returns, will already probably have dealt with tricky handwriting.

The best tip is to read the documents very slowly indeed, letter by letter, rather than word by word and certainly not sentence by sentence. You may need to transcribe (i.e. copy) the document in order to read it. Retain the original spelling and do not at first try to translate it into modern English. Begin by examining the first word and identifying each letter and then building up words and sentences from there. If a letter or word cannot be identified at first, leave a blank or put a question mark by the letter/word. The context of the other words may become apparent as time goes on. The

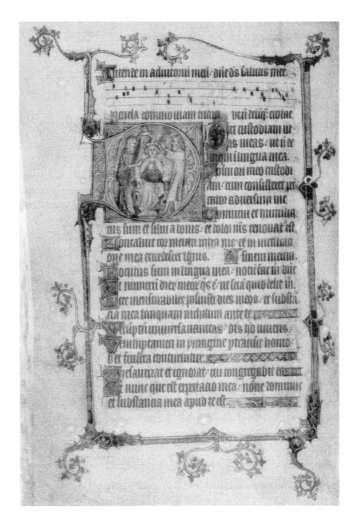

Latin Psalter, fourteenth century. Paul Lang's collection.

same word may be repeated and it may be more readable on the next occasion. Depending on what type of document it is, standard phrases will tend to appear therein. Once these have been identified, this will make reading the document easier. These may then help decipher other words in the same document.

Of course, it is easier to transcribe documents if they are in English, but even so, words are often spelt differently to modern usage. Printing helped standardize spelling, but prior to the eighteenth century spellings were variable, and words were often spelt phonetically. Furthermore, some everyday words used centuries ago have now totally fallen into disuse. An older dictionary may help with definitions. Some letters are used interchangeably, such as I and j, y and I, u and v, and f and s can be confused as they are written in a similar fashion.

Abbreviations can also cause difficulties. Medieval scribes were busy fellows and wanted to save themselves time, especially on words which appeared regularly (think of text messages on mobile phones for a modern, if ephemeral, example). These abbreviations may either involve letter(s) omitted from the middle of a word or at their end, and are indicated by a line above the word or by an apostrophe at the end. C T Martin's *The Record Interpreter* has a list of common abbreviations and Jenkinson's *Court Hand* deals with the matter, too.

Names can present a difficulty, because names are often in Latin. Johannes is used for John and Ade for Adam. The other difficulty is that, until the fifteenth century, surnames were not hereditary, and could be based on where someone lived, or their occupation or a physical feature. Names such as Will Scarlet, Much the Miller's son and Sir Guy of Gisborne spring to mind to aficionados of the Robin Hood stories. However wealthier members of society had hereditary surnames since the twelfth and thirteenth century. Likewise, names of places can be far removed from modern spellings; but there is a series of place-name dictionaries, organized by county, which list all the variant spellings.

Finally, there is no need to read every single part of the court roll (for example) which you believe your ancestor may be named on. Only that line which mentions their name is relevant to you. Therefore the ability to spot the relevant name among the others will narrow down your work considerably. Many of these documents are set out in a standard manner and some phrases will be formulaic, both of which make reading easier. The legal phraseology of most deeds can usually be safely skipped as it is irrelevant to modern researchers, as well as often being horrendously lengthy.

Initially reading old handwriting, especially if in medieval Latin, is not easy. Yet if you are to trace your ancestors back beyond the sixteenth century, it is a necessary knack to acquire, and with practice it will become less difficult. If you can take a photocopy or photographic copy of the relevant document(s), do so. You can then deal with it at home, in leisure, with reference works to hand – perhaps a knowledgeable friend can help, too, but don't expect staff to assist (they are busy with other tasks).

Appendix 2

PUBLISHED CALENDARS

In the nineteenth and early twentieth centuries, historians and archivists spent much of their time in the calendaring and publication of documents, mostly from the medieval and early modern period. These are not complete transcriptions, but are summaries of the salient points contained within the documents, with names, places and actions. Published documents are easier to read and also to copy and negate the need to see the original documents, often held at TNA. Even if the transcription is not a translation, it will still be easier to deal with, being readable and easy to photocopy. Furthermore, they are almost always well indexed by place and name.

Act Books, 1078–1228
The English Episcopal Acta project has resulted in the publication of two volumes of charters issued by the bishops of the diocese. These have been transcribed in Latin, but there is a synopsis in English for each and there is a useful index to people, places and things.

Calendar of Assizes Records (1973–95)
Sixteen volumes covering the assize records of the Home Circuit from 1558–1625.

Calendar of Various Chancery Rolls, Supplementary Close Rolls ... Preserved in the Public Record Office, AD. 1277–1326 (1912)
These are letters of instruction from the Crown and letters relating to military service.

Calendar of Chancery Warrants preserved in the Public Record Office, 1244–1326 (1927).
These are warrants under the Great Seal.

Calendar of the Charter Rolls Preserved in the Public Record Office (1903–27)
This six-volume series covers 1226–1516 and is in English.

Calendars of Charters and Rolls Preserved in the Bodleian Library
Guide to the pre-twentieth-century manuscript holdings at said library.

Calendar of the Fine Rolls (1911–62)
This twenty-two-volume series, indexed and written in English, covers 1272–1509. Fine rolls for John's reign, 1199–1216, albeit in Latin, are in *Rotuli de Oblatis et Finibus … Tempore Regis Johannis* (1835). Those for his successor, Henry III, are also in Latin, in *Excerpta et Rotuli Finium in Turri Londinensi Asservatis* (1835–6).

Calendars of Inquisition Post Mortem, 1235–1660
This is a twenty-two-volume series covering inquisitions, with some gaps, though it is an ongoing project, having begun in 1904. It has been written in English and indexed by person and place, but excludes names of jurors.

Calendars of Inquisitions Miscellaneous (Chancery) Preserved in the Public Record Office, 1218–1485 (1916–2003)
An eight-volume series covering the fate of the lands of those suspected of treason or who rebelled against the King. In English.

Inquistitions and Assessments relating to Feudal Aids, 1284–1431 (1899–1920)
This six-volume series contains a number of medieval Exchequer Books used for the assessment of taxes and subsidies. In Latin, but indexed. It is organized geographically.

Letters and Papers, Foreign and Domestic, of the Reign of Henry VIII (1862–1932)
This twenty-three-volume series is indexed and contains many references to individuals who had dealings with Henry's government in various capacities.

Calendar of the Liberate Rolls (1916–64)
This six-volume set covers most of the years of Henry III's reign, 1226–72, and concern payments to royal officials. Indexed and in English.

Memoranda Rolls
These records concern finance and property and a number have been calendared from 1199 to 1327, some by the Pipe Roll Society and some by HMSO.

Calendar of the Patent Rolls (1906–2002)
These volumes provide English summaries of the rolls from 1232–1582 and are indexed.

Calendar of Patent Rolls of the Reign of Henry III (1901–3)

Calendars of the Proceedings in Chancery in the Reign of Queen Elizabeth (1827–32)
Three-volume series.

Calendar of Signet Letters of Henry IV and Henry V (1978)
Letters written by the two monarchs, father and son, who reigned 1399–1413 and 1413–22.

Calendars of State Papers Domestic, 1509–1704
State Papers are documents either created by government or received by them. They include references to clergymen, gentry, soldiers, criminals, traitors and many others. They were transcribed and indexed and form a large series of large, weighty volumes, and can be located on the open shelves of TNA.

Calendars of Treasury Papers and Books, 1557–1745
These numerous volumes list payments to individuals for services on the monarch's or the government's business. Indexed and available on open access on TNA's shelves.

Nonarum Inquistiones in Curia Saccari (1807)
Transcriptions of the wool tax returns for 1340 for twenty-seven counties.

Pipe Rolls
Most from 1156–1221 have been calendared by the Pipe Roll Society, but others have been published by county record societies, too. They list payments to the Exchequer and the officials concerned with its administration.

The Poll Taxes of 1377, 1379 and 1381
Two volumes of transcribed tax returns (Bedfordshire to Leicestershire, then Lincolnshire to Westmorland) and a third volume as index to the first two.

Privy Council of England, Proceedings and Ordinances, 1386–1542 (1834–7) **and** *The Acts of the Privy Council of England, 1542–1631* (1890–1964)
The Privy Council was made up of the monarch's senior advisers and ministers and dealt with many different matters, including justice and land transactions. They also dealt with petitions to the monarch.

Rolls Series
This is a 255-volume series of documents, translated and transcribed,

which are relevant to British history from the time of the Romans to that of Henry VIII. It was commissioned in 1857 and work has now been completed. They should be available in larger libraries and university libraries.

Selden Society volumes
Begun in 1887 and ongoing, these annual volumes cover judicial and legal papers from the late twelfth century to the mid-sixteenth. They are indexed by name and, though originally the text was in Latin only, English translations appear in the later volumes.

Calendars produced by record societies
Most English counties have a record society which produces an annual volume of records relevant to the county's history. These could be parish registers, lists of militiamen, diaries letters, memoirs, accounts and taxation rolls and are often indexed by name. These have been in production since the nineteenth century and continue to this day. There are other record societies not limited by county, such as the Catholic Record Society, which produce similar volumes of edited records. They can be found on the shelves of TNA's library and also in county record offices and large libraries for the relevant county record series.

BIBLIOGRAPHY

There are hundreds, if not thousands of books about family history. Some are general guides to the topic and cover many different topics. Some are more specific, and tackle one area of interest in depth. I have tried to include a fair sample of what is available now (I have excluded articles in magazines), but please remember that more titles are appearing every year and information can quickly date. There are also books on genealogy from particular regions of England in the Pen and Sword Books series. There is no need to buy or even read all of these books, but if your ancestor fits into one of the categories below, they may well be worth a look. Many libraries and record offices have a selection of some of these. TNA sells many of these in its shop.

A Bevan, *Tracing your Ancestors in the National Archives* (2006)

N Barratt, *Guide to your Ancestors' Lives* (2010)

I A Baxter, *Biographical Sources in the India Office Records* (2004)

S Bourne and A H Chicken, *Records of the Church of England: A Practical Guide* (1988)

G R Breed, *My Ancestors were Baptists* (1988)

P Chambers, *How to Find your Medieval Ancestors* (2005)

P Christian, *The Genealogists' Internet* (2005)

N Currer-Briggs and R Gambien, *Huguenot Ancestry* (2001)

C Coredon and A Williams, *A Dictionary of Medieval Terms and Phrases* (2011)

W S Duck, *Examples of Handwriting, 1550–1650* (1982)

P Faithfull, *Basic Facts about Lunatics* (2002)

S Fowler, *Army Records for Family Historians* (2006)

S Fowler, *Using Poor Law Records* (2001)

S Fowler, *Tracing your Ancestors* (2011)

M Gandy, *Tracing Catholic Ancestors* (2001)

M Gandy, *Tracing Nonconformist Ancestors* (2001)

J S W Gibson, *Quarter Sessions Records for Family Historians* (1995)

J S W Gibson and A Dell, *Tudor and Stuart Muster Rolls* (1991)

J S W Gibson and A Dell, *Protestation Returns, 1641–1642 and Other Contemporary Listings* (1995)

J S W Gibson and E Hampson, *Specialist Indexes for Family Historians* (2001)

J S W Gibson and C Rogers, *Poll Books, 1696–1872* (1994)

J S W Gibson and C Rogers, *Coroners' Records* (2000)

E Gooder, *Latin for Local Historians* (1978).

K Grannum and N Taylor, *Wills and Other Probate Records: A Practical Guide* (2004)

D T Hawkings, *Criminal Ancestors, a Guide* (1996)

D Hey, *Journeys in Family History* (2004)

D Hey, *Encyclopedia of Local and Family History* (2008)

H Jenkinson, *English Court Hand*, 2 vols (1915)

J Jurskowski, C Smith and D Crook, *Lay Taxes in England and Wales, 1188-1688* (1998)

P Kershaw and M Pearsall, *Immigrants and Aliens* (2000)

W Leary, *My Ancestors were Methodists* (1999)

H Marshall, *Palaeography for Family and Local Historians* (2010)

E H Milligan and M J Thomas, *My Ancestors were Quakers* (1999)

R Paley, *Using Criminal Records* (2001)

S A Raymond, *Census, 1801–1911: A Guide for the Internet Era* (2009)

A Sherman, *My Ancestor was a Policeman* (2000)

W Spencer, *Records of the Militia and Volunteer Forces, 1757–1945* (1997)

S Wade, *Tracing your Criminal Ancestors* (2009)

C Waters, *Family History on the Net, 2011/2012* (2011)

C Webb, *Dates and Calendars for the Genealogist* (1989)

R Wenzerul, *Tracing your Jewish Ancestors? A Guide* (2008)

Finally, don't forget the monthly family history magazines available at most newsagents. These also include adverts of record agents who will, for a fee, undertake research on your behalf. Or you can contact the Association of Geneaologists and Record Agents at 29 Badger's Close, Horsham, West Sussex, RH12 5RU, and include a cheque for a list of the agents on their books. Their website is: http://www.agra.org.uk.

English History

Again, the complete book list would be very large. There are single-volume histories and there are excellent histories of particular time periods and of particular regions, towns or cities, for instance in the History Press series. Many can be found for sale in bookshops or available on the internet.

The Victoria County History series, a series begun in 1898 and still ongoing, aims to provide a detailed local history of every parish in England. The series is particularly recommended for, although incomplete, it provides a great deal of information about social, economic, religious and administrative history, complete with the whereabouts of the sources used. The series can also be seen online: http://www.british-history.ac.uk.

An excellent single volume history is K O Morgan (ed.), *A Concise History of Britain* (1992).

INDEX